Acclaim for Brent Filson's
The LEADERSHIP TALK

"What Brent Filson teaches is simple, yet profound in its implications. We need to motivate people, not have them simply do things. Instead of telling people what we want them to do, we need to understand their motivation, tap their emotion, and enlist them as cause leaders to share a dream. I keep Brent's card in my wallet to remind me of the process. Every Leadership Talk I give follows it. I used this process to enlist support in a campaign for corporate giving. As a result, we increased employee participation and realized a 10% increase in the giving rate."

> — *David Goodnight, Vice President, South America,*
> *Asia/Pacific, Lexmark International.*

"Brent's methods are tremendously valuable in driving monumental change through the leadership of others supporting your cause. Developing cause leaders has allowed ordinary teams in my organization to achieve extraordinary results."

> — *Robert Cancalosi, Global General Manager,*
> *General Electric Medical*

"Brent Filson's 'Three Trigger Motivational Process' makes the Leadership Talk all the more concrete. I refer to the wallet card frequently to keep me on course. His two-day intensive seminar is a winner!"

> — *Mark Goldman, Office of Career Development and*
> *Employee Work Life, NASA Goddard Space Flight Center*

"In my work with many cultures in many countries all over the world during the past two decades, I have encountered myriad leaders and leadership programs—but Brent's methodologies are really special. He not only focuses on having leaders consistently get actual results (not just talk about getting results), but his methods have people become engaged in profoundly human ways. Furthermore, he makes leadership and getting results a true joy!"

> — *Dr. Jeanne-Marie Col,*
> *Dept of Economic & Social Affairs, the United Nations*

More acclaim for
The Leadership Talk

"Brent Filson's leadership methods continue to be foremost in helping me get far more results at our power generating organization—and get those results in the best possible ways, by establishing an environment in which people at all levels are continually motivated to do their best."

> — *Ashton Harrilal, Supervisor, Powergen, Trinidad, West Indies*

"I've been using Brent Filson's methods for more than seven years. They get results, not only on a tactical level, but a strategic level too!"

> — *Richard Brown, President & Global General Manager,*
> *Fortune 100 Company*

"Brent Filson knows how to help others get results! His programs are proven in a variety of settings including industry, government, nonprofit, and the military, proving that the way he practices and coaches leadership can work for any organization willing to invest the time and energy necessary to influence its people to produce at their highest productivity levels."

> — *Joe Javorski, Director, Worldwide Staffing, Analog Devices*

"Brent's approach to Action Leadership is a powerful tool. I have applied his techniques in many companies and on many continents and gotten universal results. In my latest assignment, applying the principles helped improve operating margin by over 30 points."

> — *Paul Conroy, Business General Manager, Honeywell Europe*

Praise for Brent Filson's Executive Speeches

"Not for executives only! Whatever cause, policy, or product you promote, this book can help you succeed. Thoughtful. Insightful. Practical. Readable."

> — *Dr. Kathryn Clarenbach, Professor Emeritus, Political Science,*
> *University of Wisconsin, and co-founder of NOW,*
> *the National Organization for Women*

"For women, *Executive Speeches* has a hidden bonus. While discovering that speech-making can be bearable — even a kick — women get an unguarded view of the male executive mind at work."

> — *Kate Rand Lloyd, Editor-at-Large,*
> Working Woman *magazine*

The
LEADERSHIP
TALK

The Greatest Leadership Tool

Motivate People to Get More Results,
Faster Results — Continually

BRENT FILSON

WILLIAMSTOWN PUBLISHING COMPANY

Williamstown Publishing Company
P.O. Box 295
Williamstown, MA 01267

Book and cover design: Michael Brechner / Cypress House

Library of Congress Cataloging-in-Publication Data

Filson, Brent.
    The leadership talk : motivate people to get more results,
faster results, continually / Brent Filson. -- Williamstown, MA :
Williamstown Pub. Co., 2004.
    p. ; cm.
    Includes index.
    ISBN: 0-9749042-0-1
    0-9749042-1-X (pbk.)
    1. Leadership. 2. Motivation (Psychology) 3. Management.
    4. Organizational effectiveness. I. Title.
    HD57.7 .F557 2004
    658.4 / 092--dc22 0404   2004102330

Published by Williamstown Publishing Company
Printed in the Canada

2 4 6 8 9 7 5 3 1

Contents

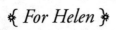

For Helen

Preface

HER BRIEF, BITTER LAUGH SAID IT ALL. I had called her to set up an appointment to meet about a leadership project I was developing for the utilities company she worked for. She said, "Sorry, Brent, I can't meet with you. I'm outta here."

"What?"

"A few hours ago, I got a call from a young man. He sounded at least ten years younger than me, maybe even younger. He said he was replacing me and wanted to schedule a meeting to iron out the details. Apparently, after fifteen years of busting my tail for this company, I'm being let go. I'll get a severance package and help finding another job."

"This was out of the blue?"

"Totally."

"And you're being replaced by one person?"

"One *young* person. Me and my whole department, the whole shebang...kaput."

Then she laughed. I realized that I had heard a laugh like that, once, when I had a summer job out of high school. I was working at a nursery for twenty-five cents an hour, where three inexperienced men, not much higher on the pay scale, were building a greenhouse. One cut off his finger with a power saw. I saw the circular blade biting through the wood—then his finger suddenly lying in the sawdust. And in the next moment, before he yelped in pain, when the first spurt of blood came out of the stump, before the wrapping of his hand in a T-shirt, before the wild drive to the hospital, he raised his hand to eye level and laughed at the farce of suddenly having four fingers instead of five. It was a brief, bitter laugh; *that's* the laugh the woman gave when she told me the news.

Looking back, I realize now that her laugh summed up the reaction of many laid-off employees I've encountered during a defining era in business. It's an era that spans roughly a quarter-century and continues today, an era of the rapid emergence and growth of global markets, the dissemination of new technologies, the radical restructuring of businesses' tables of organization, and the death of the so-called unwritten "social contract." That contract, generally assumed to have evolved spontaneously across our nation in the economic salad days after World War II, warranted that if you worked for a viable company and performed well, you'd be assured of employment until your retirement. Whether that contract truly existed isn't important here — it was *perceived* to exist, especially by those who found their jobs threatened or became jobless. Social contract or no, rafts of hard-working, skilled employees have been and are being laid off whenever companies need an extra jolt of efficiency — some in clumsy and callous ways, as was the woman at the utilities company, others in more sympathetic ways. In the early part of that era, many of the laid off, like the woman, felt duped. During the last few years, however, with the lay-off mania commonplace, a new generation of workers, more cynical, less company loyal, has entered the American workforce; talk of "social contract" has ceased, and the laid off generally accept their fate as the fruit of the natural way of things.

I had jumped into the turbulent waters of the era when, two decades ago, I was invited to write speeches as an independent contractor for a major American company. For the previous fifteen years, I had pursued a freelance writing career, tackling a variety of fiction and nonfiction subjects, except business. Despite my lack of business experience, I wrote speeches that worked, mainly because I focused on the people aspect of business: leading people, motivating people.

Though the company's CEO was just starting to become famous in global business circles, I had never heard of him. He was being widely and sharply criticized for taking the unprecedented step of stripping what he perceived to be unnecessary organizational reporting layers and making wholesale cuts in the workforce — all to get exceptional growth in the top and bottom lines. Pundits predicted he was destroying the company. He persisted, the dire predictions failed to materialize, and the stock soared. By any corporate measure, the company became one of the world's strongest. His crusade created a new blueprint for organizational competitiveness. But I was convinced then and remain convinced that, though he had gone far, he hadn't gone far enough. He had taken a big step, a necessary step, and had revitalized the company, but from my perspective, it was only a first step. A second step needed to be taken, a much more important step that might well produce more results and make that first step look as clumsy as ringing a doorbell with a cannonball. This step wouldn't have been to subtract people but to add them—not in terms of numbers but in terms of vital energy. This meant not having power over people, but power *with* people. It meant not having people simply react to changes and to their leaders' dictates but having them put their hearts into making sure the changes succeeded. After all, leaders do nothing more important than get results, and the best way they get results is not to order people to go from point A to point B, but to have those people *want to* go from A to B. Having the ability to instill that *want to* in people is a defining difference between leaders—and ultimately between organizations.

The CEO never took that next step, nor has any other company I know of. Clearly, with the sheer force of his personality, intelligence, and passions, and those of the leaders he inspired, he got results. He and a few of his lieutenants were masters at instilling *want to.* When he was in a room there was electricity in the air. He was passionate, and inspired passion in the people around him, but his passion, even the passion he inspired in his circle, isn't the point of the next step. (After all, if those in his circle weren't passionate advocates of his leadership, they'd have been outta there.) The point is, could they transfer their passion to others, and have those others transfer *their* passion—and on and on? That cascading is what separates the good results the CEO and his leaders got from the great results that they might have missed, for even greater results might have accrued if the same comprehensive, systematic, persistent efforts that had been applied to the stripping out and paring down had also been applied to tapping the hearts of the rank and file.

(I'm not talking about simply getting people motivated. Merely motivated people are useless to a business; only those people who get results are useful. The point is that skilled, motivated people have the best chance of getting results.)

Writing speeches gave me a ticket to interact with leaders at all levels in all functions in the company. I saw that the passion exhibited by up-per-echelon leaders was distributed only in sparse patches through the ranks of middle managers and supervisors. The CEO and some of his lieutenants admitted this failing. They often said that their attempts to saturate these ranks with passionately inspired leaders, the essence of the second step, was one of their toughest challenges ("Like pushing wet spaghetti," one leader said), —those attempts being ad hoc and not supported by company-wide motivational methods. The CEO directed the dissemination of training programs and the development of a world-renowned corporate university, but as helpful as such programs and the university came to be, they didn't fundamentally change the way most leaders led. Most leaders I encountered continued to adhere to an order-giving way of having people go from A to B—not the best way to reach people's hearts. They were superlative order givers—but in the end mere order givers.

I'm not saying that order-leadership should be scrapped. There are times when it's perfectly appropriate and highly motivational. I'm saying that it should be used infrequently and only at the right time, in the right way, with the right force. Few leaders I've encountered can consistently do so.

It may seem an over simplification. After all, the way leaders lead isn't simple; it encompasses the complex dimensions of being human. Still, my experience of the past two decades bears out that the cultures of all organizations I've worked in reward order giving explicitly or implicitly.

Some five years later, my speech-writing services were no longer requested. New lieutenants came aboard and mandated that leaders write their own speeches, so my run was over. I've found that when a door of opportunity closes in life, another opens somewhere. You might not see that door right away, or it might not open immediately, but it's there. So it was in my case. That new door of opportunity was there, though I had to do some kicking to get it open. I wanted to transform my speech-writing contribution into something far more valuable. Writing speeches confirmed what I'd suspected for a long time: there is a leadership / speech continuum, and for a leader to lead well, he or she must speak well, and this "speaking" transcended simply giving speeches; it involved all the talking (and listening) interactions that leaders have daily. I wanted to show that a second step could be taken by using simple, powerful, daily-repeatable talking methods. I wanted to develop such methods myself. I knew it wouldn't be easy—an "impossible dream," many leaders told me. I knew that to succeed I would have to draw on not just my speech-writing resources but on the resources I had used for all my other writings, the things I'd learned over the decades about research, communication, analysis, and ways of tapping the subconscious. Further, I would have to draw on my own leadership experiences and those that I had witnessed, going all the way back to my days in the military.

So, I went to the mountain, my private mountain, a nineteenth-century New England farmstead that became my twentieth-century farmstead of the mind and spirit, and set to work. I will touch on some aspects of how I developed the methods in Chapter 1. Suffice to say that I took as my challenge Spinosa's dictum, "All excellent things are as difficult as they are rare," and worked round-the-clock, helped by meditation, exercise, and family ties. Emulating the Yankee yeomen who had once farmed my rock-strewn plot, I stuck to the practical. I formulated the methods in the rocky bottomland of real time, real-world demands, helping leaders of all ranks and functions in many companies, leaders who urgently needed to get results and were impatient with anything that didn't work. I saw that many shared the same problems, were getting only a fraction of the results they were capable of, and struggled in their jobs and careers, some failing tragically and unnecessarily, others simply doing less well than they were capable of doing. They struggled not because they lacked intelligence, knowledge, or skills, but because they lacked rigorous, repeatable leadership methods to help them consistently win the heartfelt commitment of other people.

I saw that some of the most troubled leaders were the super-stars—leaders who know everything, but nothing else. In terms of winning that cascading commitment, they were afflicted with a virulent leadership virus called "good enough." They believed they were pretty great, so they didn't feel the need to change their outlook and actions even when it came to contemplating the cascade, let alone launching it. In their success, they were failing disastrously —not knowing that they did not know.

The upshot is the Leadership Talk. It is not a way of talking, a funda-mentally new way of leading, which, paradoxically, is as old as history. It's not a style of leadership; it's not a technique. It's a way of life. For if our leadership is not a way of life, then that leadership and our lives are diminished.

How to Use This Book

You can build a better career using Leadership Talks, and *using* this book, not simply reading it, you can give better and better Leadership Talks.

Here's how: First, understand the reasoning behind the structure. The book is divided into two sections, Concepts and Application. The Concepts section delves into the essential ideas of the Leadership Talk. The Application section shows you how to actually develop and deliver the Talk. The idea is for you to get a thorough grounding in the concepts before delivering your first Leadership Talk. With this in mind, read the book straight through once, and then apply the practice procedures. The practice procedures are not Leadership Talks. The Talk is the punch, the procedures the motor muscles that propel it. Having applied the practice procedures for a few days or weeks—or at least until you feel that you've learned their lessons—then move to the Application section.

Let's examine both sections in detail. The Concepts section contains the philosophy of The Leadership Talk and the key process to realizing it: the Three-trigger Motivational Process (TMP). The triggers are Needs, Belief, and Action. Each trigger is divided into three learning parts: Dialogue, Lessons, and Practice.

The Dialogue part shows how a facet of the Leadership Talk was developed in a challenging situation. I've used dialogues to help impart the basics of the Leadership Talk, not only because interaction and relationship are potent teaching methods but also because it was through dialogues with leaders of all types that I worked out those basics.

The dialogues are not verbatim. I've taken the liberty of putting into speakers' mouths words that weren't actually spoken but faith-

fully represent what was said. I didn't take extensive notes during my
conversations. If I had recorded our interactions and then transcribed
them in total, the text would have been much longer—and less effective.
This book has one goal: to help you understand, develop, and deliver
Leadership Talks. It provides not the full mass of experiences that took
place over weeks and months, but the tincture of those experiences,
to expedite your learning and eventually doing. Most of the dialogues
came from my conversing with actual leaders. However, I've also used
the composite technique in several sections, because I want to protect
the privacy of the leaders involved and because my combining the
interactions I had with several leaders into a single composite person
and composite situations provides far richer instructional material
than any encounter with one actual person or situation. I don't intend
to communicate the truth of actual people, but the deeper truths of
practical knowledge.

The Lessons part of the Concepts section details the pertinent points
derived from that dialogue. Though a given dialogue may focus on an
organizational function or leadership rank you might not be familiar
with, its leadership principles are universally applicable. Even though I
may be having a dialogue with a plant manager, line supervisor, CEO,
or sales and marketing leader or financial leader, and you've never held
nor expect to hold any of those positions, the dialogues will nonetheless
apply directly to your personal leadership challenges. The principles of
the Leadership Talk transcend organizational function. This was brought
home to me in a forceful way when, some years ago, I was giving a seminar on the Leadership Talk to executives from a variety of companies.
One was from a utility, another from an engineering thermoplastics
company, another from a soup company, another an insurance company,
and another from a telecommunications company. One sold electrons,
one sold polymer molecules, one sold food, one sold whole life, and one
sold digital technologies. *Yet all of them shared precisely the same leadership challenges.* This single experience has been borne out in countless
encounters I've had with leaders during the past two decades. So, the
dialogues and their lessons are not one-of-a-kind situations useful only

to the leaders I spoke with, but represent problems common to leaders of all ranks and functions—icons that can yield continually fresh solutions throughout your career.

The Practice part of the Concepts section shows you how to put those lessons into action. Note that each Practice part is composed of three phases of action. Tackle each phase one at a time. Don't skip a phase. You'll find that once you follow the instruction sequences in this book, the Leadership Talk is relatively simple to learn—though it takes years to master. The good is the enemy of the best; so, no matter how good you get, you can always get better. Commit yourself to a lifetime of continuous improvement. That commitment begins now with your making the effort to build a lasting foundation.

The Application section will show you practical ways to repeatedly develop and deliver Leadership Talks. This section is divided into five parts: "Bringing It All Together," "The Motivational Elements," "The Leadership Talk Process," "The Interactive Leadership Talk," and "Doing It."

Regarding "Bringing It All Together," encountering the Leadership Talk for the first time is much like free-fall parachuting. A newcomer to the Talk may find that the learning can be unsettling at times—a "What have I gotten myself into?" experience. You might have questions that can be answered only at the end of the book when the ideas coalesce. Innately, you already know the basic concepts of the Talk. (I'm here to simply help lead you there.) The free-fall feeling is a natural reaction of your mind trying to establish new linkages between old understandings. In the "Bringing it all Together" part of the Application section, the "parachute" will open and you will land; and when you do, you'll find yourself in a new leadership place, surrounded by career-building opportunities.

In the "Interactive" part, I'll show you how to deliver the Leadership Talk in those all-important give-and-take encounters with others. Finally, in the "Doing It" part, I'll show you how you can use and teach the Leadership Talk daily throughout your entire career.

An appendix provides sample defining moments and outcomes of the Leadership Talks that derive from the dialogues in the book, and a glossary helps define the concepts.

I can think of no better way to achieve career success than to be devoted to giving Leadership Talks, so don't let a little free falling deter you. Let's jump!

Section 1: Concepts

Einstein, the Universe, and Leadership

LONG BEFORE I CROSSED PATHS WITH THE COMPANY I talked about in the preface, I began asking the questions that would take me in search of the wellsprings of leadership, and from those sources ultimately develop the Leadership Talk. In the military, I saw that there were leaders whom the troops would die for—and others whom the troops wanted to have die for them! I wondered what made the former different from the latter, and if those differences could be learned and put into action. I arrived at no hard answers, and then help came from an unexpected source—Albert Einstein. I happened to read about Einstein's three-decade quest to formulate the Unified Field Theory of the universe, a theory that seeks to unify all the known forces of the universe into a single, coherent formulation. Reading about his quest gave new focus to mine.

Einstein's special and general theories applied to our universe on the macro level, on scales of astronomical distance. However, on the micro level, in the world of atoms, electrons, and far smaller particles, matter behaves in altogether different ways. Quantum mechanics shows that matter on these ultramicroscopic levels doesn't have the smooth, geometric features we know on the macro level. It's a seething, violent world, so baffling that a noted physicist observed that *anyone who claims to understand quantum mechanics is really ignorant of it.* Yet both the macro and micro, worlds that seemingly have no relationship to one another, comprise our reality. Einstein proposed to show how those two worlds are interrelated and interdependent. He called it his Unified Field Theory. (Some physicists called it TOE—theory of everything.) For thirty years, he tried to develop such a theory—and ultimately failed.

I saw Einstein's failure as triumph. In dreaming the impossible dream, he had made the seemingly impossible a practical quest. Today, physicists around the world are still working on the theory, and the common perception is that the development of a Unified Field Theory will happen in the not-too-distant future.

I'm no physicist. My quest wasn't in the realm of matter, energy, motion, and force, but in the realm of leadership. In my small way, I yearned to come up with my own theory, the Unified Field Theory of Leadership. Just as Einstein aspired to reduce the complexities of the macro and micro worlds to unified equations, I aspired to reduce the complexities of leadership to simple propositions that, when put into action, would enable any leader to consistently get more results by inspiring *want to* in other people.

The Unified Field Theory of Leadership

I don't write books simply about what I know; I write books because I want to find out. I decided to write a book about the Unified Field Theory of Leadership to find out if it indeed existed, and if so, in what content and form.

I first looked into communication, thinking *After all, it's not enough for one to be a leader; one must communicate leadership. Communication isn't about moving information. It's about getting people moving by using information. It's about transferring our convictions to others.*

So, I sent out hundreds of letters to leaders in organizations around the nation. I asked simply, "How do you communicate?"

The deluge of responses I waited for didn't come. I got a trickle instead. The few leaders who responded said, in effect, *I know communication is important. But what exactly is communication? How do we know if we're doing it well, or if we're doing it poorly?*

Then I had a head-on crash with a Blinding Flash of the Obvious. From one CEO, I received a letter that marked a defining moment in my career. The letter said simply, "You asked, 'How do you communicate?'

It's the wrong question! The key question in everybody's career isn't 'How do you communicate?' It's 'How do you give speeches?'"

I'm not just talking about giving speeches from a podium. I'm talking about speaking—for the purposes of this book, *talking*—there's a crucial difference. Leaders must constantly be talking. I call it the "leadership/talk continuum," and if you can't talk well, you can't lead well.

So I sent out a new letter to CEOs, asking simply, "How do you talk?" This time, the deluge: many CEOs wrote back, saying, in effect, that speaking/talking was vital to their career advancement.

The CEO of a large Midwestern insurance company told me that, fifteen years earlier, when he'd walked in the door on his first day as brand-new CEO of a company whose sales had been plummeting for months, the communications director handed him a microphone and said, "Please speak to the employees over the PA system. Boost their morale." The CEO told me that he reached for the mike, then stopped. In that moment, he made a career-changing decision.

"Brent, I decided not to take that mike. I decided I wasn't going to speak to them over the PA system. I decided that I would talk with them face to face."

His company consisted of some 16,000 employees spread over thirty-two floors. He went out and spoke to them in groups of three to ten. It took seven months. "I turned that company around by turning the employees of that company around."

When he told me that, I began to get an inkling of Unified Field Theory of Leadership Success.

This was my reasoning: clearly, that CEO had to get results: He had to get the company profitable again, or he wouldn't be a CEO for long. The Unified Field Theory had something to do with getting results. So, the first proposition of Unified Field Theory was:

1. Organizational Success is a Function of Leaders Achieving Results

Obviously, organizations are formed to achieve results. Leaders channel the activities of those organizations toward those achievements. But leaders don't get results in a vacuum. Results come from a Latin root, "to spring back." A leader must lead somebody to get results. After all, the CEO turned the company around by turning *the people* around. So, a leader doesn't just get results; results "spring back," they also get the leader.

2. Leaders Get Results By Having People Get Results

I reasoned that there are two ways we can "have" people get results: the first is to order them. In this sense, "have" is an active verb. The second way is to motivate them. In this sense, "have" is a passive verb. Thinking about it, I understood that in its passive sense, "have" is a far more powerful means of getting results than in its active sense.

3. The Best Way to Have People Get Results is to Motivate Them

Motivation bridges the gap between understanding and devotion. Yet in my work with leaders over the years, I discovered that many misunderstood the concept and application of motivation. If motivation was going to be incorporated into the Unified Field Theory of Leadership Success, I had to understand motivation at its roots. To do so, I asked four questions about it: What is motivation? Who does motivation? What animates motivation? What's the best way to make motivation happen?

What is motivation?

The word starts with "mo," which comes from an Old Latin base that helps form such words as "momentum," "movement," "motion," and "mobilization,"—words that embody physical action. Motivation isn't what people think or feel; it's what people *do*. Motivation is physical action.

Further, motivation is not inspiration. Inspiration comes from the Latin for "to breathe in" or "to breathe religious or divine feeling into."

The word originates in the activities of the oracle of Delphi, the priestess of the god Apollo, who purportedly communicated the god's messages to humans. She sat before a fissure in the earth, breathed in vapors rising from the fissure (recent geological findings suggest the vapors were ethylene), and so was "inspired" to prophesy. For instance, nearly 2,500 years ago, as the Persians invaded Greece, she prophesied that only a wall of wood could save Greece. She couldn't, of course, build the navy that defeated the Persians at the battle of Salamis. The Greeks had to take that action. Inspiration, then, is what people think and feel. Motivation is what people actually do. I reasoned then that motivating people to get results involved having them take physical action—not the physical action connected with bands playing, flags waving, and people singing and cheering, but the quiet, often unseen physical action that gets the job done, that gets results.

Who does motivation?

I then wondered how that physical action was triggered. My question was directed at the psychological basis of motivation. The English language misses the mark regarding motivation. It describes motivation in terms of an active verb, something the motivator does to someone else. This may be syntactically true, but it's psychologically false.

The Leadership Talk is based on a principle as old as history and new as now: *When a people need to accomplish great deeds, a leader first has to gather them together and talk from the heart.*

Does that leader motivate the people, as our language denotes, or do the people, seeing and hearing the leader, motivate themselves? I concluded it was the latter, that nobody can motivate anybody to do anything. Leaders communicate—the people motivate. They motivate themselves. The motivator and the motivated are the same person. The fact that our language embodies an erroneous psychological dynamic regarding motivation creates a trap for leaders. They get caught when they think they're in control of motivation. The way out of the trap, or the way not to fall into it in the first place, is to understand that motivation is not the leader's choice. It's the people's choice. Motivation can only take place in the realm of their free choice. To understand then how to motivate people, leaders must understand how to create an environment in which those people make the choice to motivate themselves.

What animates motivation?

I looked for the answer in the root again. A Latin root forms the basis for motivation; another word shares that root, the word "emotion." When it comes to emotion, however, there's a slight difference in the root, and that difference defines a world of difference in leadership. The Latin root of "emotion" means not just "to move" but also "to move out from." Emotions are not only within us, but can also move out from us, by way of our physical responses, to affect our environment. With both *emotion* and *motivation* sharing the same root, I reasoned that the concepts are related in principle and function, and that the relationship is a causal one. Emotion gives function and meaning to motivation. People are motivated to take action only when their emotions are engaged. It's not a linear but a circular process: emotions trigger motivation, and motivation triggers emotions.

What is the best way to motivate people?

That CEO provided the answer: He didn't speak to the employees over the PA system, he talked with them face to face. Speaking briefly over the PA system would have been the slow route to their becoming motivated. Though it took him months to speak to them, that was the fast route. Face-to-face speech is the fastest and most effective way to motivate people.

Notice that I'm using "motivation" as an active verb. For the sake of clarity and consistency, I'm going to apply its common usage throughout this book. However, from now on, when I use the word "motivation," I expect that you'll understand it within the context of the preceding observations.

Here, then, are the propositions of the Unified Field Theory of Leadership Success:

1. Organizational success is a function of leaders directing those organizations to achieve results.
2. Leaders direct organizations to achieve results by having people get those results.
3. The best way to have people get results is not to order them but motivate them.
4. Motivation is physical action.
5. Motivation is not what leaders do to people, but what people do to themselves.
6. Motivation is triggered by emotion.
7. Motivation happens best through face-to-face speech.

These propositions form the organizing philosophy of the Leadership Talk. I suggest you think them through. Unless you agree with them, you'll have a difficult time understanding and giving Leadership Talks.

The Leadership Talk, however, is not simply philosophy, but a practical way of leading and a practical way of living. Let's go to the key process that can help you put that philosophy to work.

The Eight Needs Questions

HERE'S AN IMPORTANT DISTINCTION that will help you understand how to instill *want to* in other people. As a leader, you do more than speak—you talk. When you speak, people often simply listen. But when you talk, you have an informal yet potentially more powerful interchange with them, a give and take. You talk with people in meetings, and across desks, and in hallways, and in conference rooms. You talk at lunch. You talk fifteen, twenty, twenty-five times every day. These interactions provide you with most of the best opportunities to be a successful leader—but many leaders spend their whole careers giving the wrong talks!

How do you realize the full potential of your talking interactions every day? One way is through the use of processes. A process is a series of mental or physical steps that produce an intended outcome. Process transforms thought into action and directs that action toward specific ends.

A key process of the Leadership Talk is the Three-trigger Motivational Process (TMP). It should be used many times daily, before, during, and after we talk.

It's this: Before you talk, ask three questions. If you answer no to any of them, you should not talk.

- Do you know the audience's *needs?*
- Can you bring deep *belief* to what you say?
- Can you have the audience take *action?*

These questions are not meant to be stumbling blocks but stepping-stones. If you can't answer yes, work on the answers until you can. Let's analyze each question.

Do you know the audience's needs?

Why are people's needs important in terms of the Leadership Talk? They're not—if you simply want to order them to go from point A to point B. In the zero-sum game of order-leadership, the needs of the person ordering are more important than the needs of the people being ordered. But the Leadership Talk is not an order dynamic; it's a motivational dynamic. People being ordered may do what they're told, but will they do it in the best way possible? After all, they might resent the order and not carry it out well. Or they might carry out the order well, but then stop and wait for the next order. Clearly, the better way is not to order people to achieve results, but to have them want to achieve results. Making that *want to* happen daily must be your career *have to*.

We can't trigger that *want to* consistently unless we identify and understand needs. *People's needs are people's reality.* Without understanding their needs, without interacting with them within the framework of those needs, we can't give a Leadership Talk, simply because we fail to come to grips with the only reality that matters to them—theirs.

What exactly are needs? Volumes have been written about human need, but for purposes of the Leadership Talk, let's understand need as essence and as awareness. Regarding need as essence, need is a lack of something considered necessary. A need is not a want. A want is a lack of something that's not particularly necessary. A want is a "nice to have." A need is a "must have." Furthermore, a need involves an emotional response. A need doesn't just prompt emotion; a need *is* emotion. Finally, this need / emotion is a problem seeking a solution. To understand need within the context of the Leadership Talk, we must understand the lack, the emotion, and the problem. These three are one, each in itself the whole need. None of the three can exist without the others. As you go through this book and learn how to put together a Leadership Talk, you'll see the importance of understanding this need / emotion / problem continuum.

Regarding need as awareness, the needs we identify in our audience can be divided into needs they're aware of and needs they're unaware of. Knowing the difference can greatly impact how we relate to the audience in terms of motivating them to be our cause leaders. For instance, before definitive medical information on smoking came out, the American public didn't know that the activity caused cancer and many other ailments, so there was no national crusade against smoking. Only when such detailed information came to light, making people aware of the need not to smoke, did the crusade against smoking get up to speed. In this book, you'll see how the audience's awareness (or lack thereof) of their need will define and propel motivation.

How do we go about understanding people's needs? First, we must identify what those needs are. The best way is simply to ask—ask yourself and, of course, the people. In several of my previous books, I used an eight-question guide that many leaders are using today. Recently, I met a fast-rising executive in the airport. I hadn't seen him in the several years since he took my seminar. He pulled out the wallet card and said, "I ask the eight questions many times a day every day." If you're serious about giving Leadership Talks, you must do the same.

The Needs Questions

What is changing for the audience?
Whom would the audience rather have talking to them besides you?
What action does the audience want to take?
What does the audience feel?
What does the audience fear?
What is the audience's major problem?
What makes the audience angry?
What does the audience dream?
We'll examine each question in detail by considering a dialogue I had with a leader regarding a specific challenge that leader faced.

Question 1: What is changing for the audience?

The first truth of motivation is change—the rock on which the Leadership Talk is built. We can't give a Leadership Talk unless we first have an appreciation of: A. What we think is changing in the environment in which we are leading; and B. What the audience thinks is changing in that environment.

The word "appreciation" is vital. I'm not saying that we simply understand what's changing. Appreciation goes beyond understanding. When we understand something, we apprehend clearly its character, nature, and subtleties. But when we appreciate something, we become fully aware of its value, its price.

Here's an example of appreciation. It started with what seems like a petty dispute, but like many such disputes in organizations, it pointed to deeper contradictions that were impeding results. A manufacturing plant manager said, "My old boss stayed away from me. He let me do my job. The new boss is always in my office. He's in my face, demanding why haven't I done this, why haven't I done that. He won't let up. He needs to get out of my office."

"Why don't you tell him to get out?"

"I could. I could tell him in a nasty way—or a nice way. But why do I have to tell him? Why doesn't he get it on his own?"

"Maybe telling him to get out—in whatever way—isn't the best way."

"What's a better way?"

"The Leadership Talk."

"How?"

"The 'how' is in the function of the Talk. That function is always to motivate people to take action for results—and not just results, but more results, faster, on a continual basis. Results are limitless; those who don't understand that don't understand the Leadership Talk."

"How can I motivate him?"

"The first step is to recognize that you can't motivate him to do anything. Only he can motivate himself to get out of the office. And if he does, isn't that better than your telling him?"

"Of course!"

"The next step is to identify the needs that will drive motivation. People are only motivated through needs. A person who needs nothing can't be motivated to do anything. Since only your boss can motivate himself, whose needs would provide the motivational incentives?"

"His, of course."

"So, it's obvious. He's not the problem—*you* are."

"Me? *He's* in *my* office. I'm not in *his* office!"

"You're the problem because you have the wrong perception of what's changing for your boss. Only when you change your perceptions will you start having your boss change. Let me ask you, why is your boss in your office a lot?"

"He wants me to cut costs in our manufacturing processes. He's a one-note Johnny. 'Cut costs! Cut costs!' I guess he thinks I'll get the point if he's in my face about it. Wrong! I've gotten the point. I agree with him. But let's go back to what you just said. Why am I the problem?"

"Look at the words you used to define the situation. You said, 'My boss needs to get out of my office.'"

"Of course!"

"But is that what your boss really needs, or is that what *you* need?"

"He needs… well, maybe you're right. Let me rephrase it: *I* need to get him out of my office."

"And he really needs…"

"Cost cuts."

"In fact, his career might hinge on costs being cut."

"Absolutely."

"What just happened between you and me is pivotal. Let's look at it. What did you tell me at first?"

"That my boss needs to get out of my office."

"What do you understand now?"

"That's not his need. That's *my* need."

"What's his need?"

"To have costs cut."

"That shift you made, from perceiving your needs as his needs, to clearly understanding his needs, is the first step in developing a Leadership Talk. Look, many leaders make the same mistake: they see what they think is changing for their audience in terms of what's changing for themselves. It's a mistake that hampers their ability to get results.

Having your audience make the choice to be motivated starts with your first understanding change from your audience's perspective. Of course, sometimes the changes that the audience faces are the changes that you face, but when they're different, you must clearly separate the two areas of change. You must understand the difference and appreciate precisely what those changes are from the audience's perspective. You might not agree with what your audience perceives is changing. That's O.K. At this point in developing the Leadership Talk, we're not trying to put a value on those changes, nor are we changing their perceptions. We're simply identifying those perceptions. Look at your boss: only when you understand what's changing for him—from his perspective—can you begin to appreciate the true reality you're facing. Now, what's changing for your boss?"

"*He* has a new boss, our new CEO. His boss is expecting a lot more results than the previous CEO did. And he's cutting costs big time. That means that resources are being taken away from my boss. So, what's changing for my boss is higher expectations and fewer resources!"

"You're close, but no prize. Remember: it's not enough that you simply understand what's changing for your boss. You must *appreciate* what's changing."

"O.K., you said that *appreciation* takes in the value of the change, or the price my boss sees that he has to pay in dealing with the change."

"Go on."

"I see! The price he may think he has to pay is failure. Draw a circle around all of those changes and I see that my boss may be thinking that he's being set up to fail trying to meet the expectations of his boss. Higher expectations, less resources, that's a prescription for failure—at least in my boss's eyes."

"You've hit it. You have finally appreciated what's changing for your boss. Clearly, we don't have a Leadership Talk developed yet; but without this appreciation, you can't develop the Talk. The lesson is clear: In answering the first question, make the effort to go to the root emotion by appreciating the change your audience is encountering, not from your standpoint, but from your audience's. You might not think that it's the right change to be focusing on now, but that doesn't matter at this point. The goal now is to appreciate its value for your audience, and the price that the audiences thinks will have to be paid to meet the challenges of the change."

For a summary of how this Leadership Talk turned out, see Appendix B.

Lessons

Before giving a Leadership Talk, see the change in the challenge: What was it? What is it? What is it becoming? The plant manager couldn't see what he didn't see. He saw his boss in his office, but did not at first see the changes taking place that prompted the boss's presence. When he identified, analyzed, and began dealing with those changes, he saw that the boss being there wasn't a pain but an opportunity. Change is just another word for opportunity.

Be clear about the difference between what *you* see changing and what *your audience* sees changing. If you both see the same changes, that's fine. But if you both see different changes, then understand precisely what that difference is. Don't mix up the two. Leaders often fail to achieve the results they're capable of because they think they see change through the same eyes as their audience. Not until the plant manager began seeing change from his boss's perspective did he start taking leadership to deal with that change, and through that leadership, begin achieving more results, faster, continually.

Appreciate the change by realizing the value your audience places on it, and the price they think they'll have to pay to meet the challenge of that change. The plant manager not only had to identify the change, but also appreciate it before he could effectively deal with it. After all, if the value we give to ourselves doesn't begin with the value we give to our audience, we sell ourselves cheap; and the value we give to them begins with the answer to this question.

Get to the root of what your audience believes is changing. The plant manager thought the boss was in his office simply because he wanted to keep close tabs on him—which was true up to a point. But when he came to understand that there were deeper and more important reasons for his boss being there, he was ready to start taking action that would deal with the situation. That seemingly small redirection in focus ultimately led to a big increase in results.

We best know change by being changed. We best take control of change by taking leadership in change. We best take leadership in change by getting cause leaders for change (see Appendix B).

Question 2: Whom would the audience rather have talking to them besides you?

Leaders come to grief when they think that just because they're speaking, others are listening. The truth is, people only truly listen when they want to hear.

Grief was making a beeline for an executive I was working with—mainly because he hadn't asked and answered this question. His boss, a renowned CEO, was pushing a major quality initiative through the entire corporation of some 350,000 employees. The executive's mission was to introduce the CEO's initiative to the assembled leaders of a large division. When he told me that he intended to describe the initiative and then show a video of the CEO talking it up, I replied that he was about to get a good dose of misery.

"Why?"

"Clearly, you have to describe the initiative. And you have to communicate your CEO's commitment to it. But if you stop right there, shake hands with grief, because those leaders don't want to hear from you."

"You mean that unless that audience would rather hear from me than the CEO, *my* Leadership Talk will fizzle?"

"Yes."

"But that'll never happen. He's the CEO!"

"It not only can happen, it *must* happen. Let me put it this way: if people in an organization always want to hear only from the top leadership and not from their immediate leaders, what does that say about that organization?"

"That the immediate leaders have little power."

"They're mostly messengers?"

"Yes."

"And what's the Leadership Talk all about?"

"Getting results."

"Just results?"

"Getting more results, faster, continually."

"And what's the best way to do that?"

"By taking leadership action."

"Can a messenger motivate people to take leadership action?"

"Not likely."

"So what's your challenge?"

"To have them want to listen to *me*, me as a leader, not a messenger, meaning at that moment they should want to hear from me and not our CEO! Brother, I'm in trouble!"

"No, you're in great shape. You've taken the first positive step. You've come to understand the reality of the situation. Most leaders don't take this first step. They think their reality is the audience's reality. They think that because they're speaking, people are listening intently. But those people usually aren't listening—unless they want to hear."

"How do we get them wanting to hear?"

"The answer is in the realm of value, specifically, the value that they perceive you can bring to them. What is that value?"

"I'm telling them what the CEO wants."

"You're back to positioning yourself as a messenger. Anybody can tell them that, give handouts, show a video. I'm not talking about that. I'm talking about what value *you yourself* bring to them."

"Usefulness. They must see me as useful to them."

"How?"

"I'm useful to them when I'm helping them solve their problems."

"What problem of theirs can you solve?"

"How am I supposed to know? They have lots of problems, individually and as a group."

"That's true. Every audience you talk to has many problems, both at work and in their personal lives, and if you can't identify and understand those problems, you can't give a Leadership Talk."

"Okay, they're overloaded at work as it is. Here comes this initiative. They're wondering how they're going to have time to tackle it, wondering if they can succeed in doing it, and wondering if I really know my stuff."

"And how can you—not your CEO, *you yourself,* bring solutions to their problems?"

"I see. If I'm helping bring solutions to their real problems, then they'll see me as key to their success—and they'll *want to* hear. Now I understand, Brent, that as a leader, you can spend a career asking the wrong questions. 'Whom would they rather have speaking to them?' is one of the right questions. Now I have to come up with some answers."

For a summary of how this Leadership Talk turned out, see Appendix B.

Lessons

The difference between leaders is price—the price that they can have others choose to pay for their (the leaders') cause. But people won't be willing to pay the price unless they want to listen to you. If they'd rather have someone else speaking, you're in trouble. But you're in worse trouble if you're unaware that they don't want you there. Don't talk until you first answer this question—or at least try to answer it. Just having the executive move from not asking the question (and not knowing that he ought to), to asking it made a world of difference in the ultimate outcome of his Leadership Talk.

Don't be discouraged by your answer. The fact that the executive came to understand that the audience didn't want to hear from him was an important first step in his understanding their reality. Without this knowledge, he would have been in a leadership penalty box. Using this knowledge, he could begin to have them see him as a leader, not a messenger, and have them be more open to wanting to hear him out.

Their perceiving you as a messenger is unacceptable. If you're a leader, they must perceive you as a leader; otherwise, you will not motivate them (to motivate themselves) to make the choice to be your cause leaders.

The key to changing their perceptions lies in the value that you bring to them. That value is linked to solutions. They'll see you as a leader when you can help provide solutions to their needs—solutions that embody concrete remedies and actions.

That change in their perception of your role may have to come during your Leadership Talk. In fact, a good portion of that Talk may be devoted to making such a change happen. For instance, the executive had to devote the first part of his Talk to getting out in the open their feeling that they really wanted the CEO speaking to them (see Appendix B).

When your audience wants to hear from someone other than you, identify who, they want to hear from and the precise reasons why. The executive knew that his audience would rather have the CEO speaking to them because:

1. This initiative was coming directly from the CEO.

2. The CEO made it clear that their careers depended upon its being carried out.

3. The CEO was a charismatic, world-renowned leader who always got them motivated when he spoke. However, being a leader entails not only knowing who you are, but also knowing who you aren't. The executive knew that he couldn't offer what the CEO offered, but he knew also that there were solutions he could help bring that the CEO couldn't (see Appendix B).

Question 3: What action does the audience want to take?

A supervisor was faced with a common leadership challenge—mainly because she hadn't asked this question. She had recently been transferred to a thirty-year-old plant that was struggling to compete against much newer plants, and was put in charge of eight older men. She told me, "They're a close-knit group, and suspicious of outsiders. They've been working together for more than twenty years. I'm supposed to get them to change their old ways of doing things to get more operating efficiencies, but it's not happening. I talk with them, they agree that they have to change, but they go right back to doing what they've always done."

"Why?" I asked.

"I don't know."

"You *do* know. I haven't yet met a leader who doesn't have answers to the problems. And the answer, at least the material to get the answer, is always linked to answers to the Eight Needs Questions. Let's look at the third question. What action do they want to take at the time you talk?"

"They want to listen to me."

"Are you sure?"

"Of course! I've got them together. And I'm talking."

"But do they really want to hear to you?"

"They'd better—I'm their supervisor."

"Look at it this way: they've been doing practically the same things for more than two decades. Now management says they have to change. And here you come, shot at them out of a management cannon. They know you've been sent to get them to change. They might tell you they'll change, but do they really *want* to change?"

"I'm beginning to wonder."

"So what action do they want to take when you're talking to them?"

The supervisor was silent. Then she said, "Maybe they don't want to be there when I speak. If they see me as an outsider, and they really don't want to change, then, when I speak to them, maybe they'd rather be somewhere else."

"Where?"

"Back on their jobs."

"Doing what?"

"What they've always done."

"True motivation is not what they do when you're around them, but what they do when you're not there. Up till now, you thought that if they told you they agreed with you, they really did agree with you. But you probably got the old head fake: people nodding *yes* on the outside but saying *no* on the inside. If you had really asked this question *before* you spoke to them, what would your answer have been?"

"I don't know. I'll have to think about it. I never asked myself this question. And it's the question I should have asked!"

"What's the Chinese proverb about the thousand-mile journey?"

"It starts with a single step. I had taken a single step, all right. In fact, I'd taken a lot of steps. I was going full speed ahead—but the wrong way! Somehow, I've got to get this group not just to agree to change but to be *change leaders*—to take action and lead action for change. I realize now that I don't have change leaders, I've got change *mutineers*. They were giving me the old head fake, and I was going for it!"

For a summary of how this Leadership Talk turned out, see Appendix B.

Lessons

Even when your audience seems to be listening to you, they often want to take action—whether or not you or they consciously know it. They might want simply to hear you out (listening, or even not listening, is action), or want to get away from you. They might want to offer their assistance or rally people against you. Until we spoke, the supervisor hadn't considered this—and was missing out on tapping a rich vein of motivational raw material.

There's a big difference between the action people take when they *have to change* and the action they take when they get to change. In the supervisor's case, moving her workers from having to change to getting to change was, in part, a function of her understanding the physical action they wanted to take when she spoke to them. When she saw that her old way of speaking to them was motivating them to not change at all, to take physical action that was essentially a deception, she took the first steps in giving a true Leadership Talk.

Since you can't read their thoughts, you can't know precisely what action they want to take, but that's not as important in the development of your Leadership Talk as engaging in the questioning process. The fact that the supervisor became aware of the head fake changed the way she interacted with them. Without that knowledge, she was trying to get results the hard way. With the knowledge, she began to have them make the choice to change, which was the easy way to get results and a lot more of them. Faced with the easy way and the hard way of getting results, most leaders choose the latter, thinking it's the former. Answering this question helps make the hard easy.

Three factors contribute to the action your audience wants to take: resources, stakes, and status quo:

1. Resources

Identify what resources your audience has, their willingness to commit them to you, and the obstacles to their carrying out that commitment. Those resources can include their time, their skills, their networking connections, their influence with others, and finally, their leadership. By not dealing with the question "What action does the audience wanted to take?", the supervisor misidentified the resources she needed from them and that they were willing to give her. She thought she simply had to get their agreement, whereas she really needed their *leadership* in making change happen. Leadership is the most important resource people can give, as well as the most difficult for you to get.

2. Stakes

Stakes define what can be gained or lost. You can't give an effective Leadership Talk unless you and the audience agree on what's at stake regarding the issue you both face. Stakes are so important that a Leadership Talk may be needed to simply get that agreement. If you and your audience can't agree on the importance of the action they need to take, they'll seldom take the action you want. A "stakes gap" separated the supervisor and her workers. On the supervisor's side, she knew that if the workers didn't change, they'd continue to impair their plant's ability to compete. On the workers' side, they felt that if they did change, they'd be jeopardizing their ability to do their jobs well, and would be kowtowing to management's whims. It was a case of people wanting to do the old wrong things in the right way, rather than the new right things in the temporarily wrong way. The stakes gap was clear, but the supervisor made a common mistake: she neglected to identify the gap, let alone close it. (Closing means getting that crucial agreement.) Without such identification and closure, the workers would head fake their way to not changing at all. As a leader, you'll continually run up against stakes gaps that you must continually close. In fact, some stakes gaps are so important that failing to close them will result in the utter failure of your Leadership Talk. I call these "killer gaps."

3. Status Quo

Status quo is the existing state or condition of things. Regarding the Leadership Talk, the status quo is always wrong, simply because it doesn't exist—it's an illusion. I'm not drawing a philosophical fine point. The fact that the status quo doesn't exist is a practical reality that cuts to the marrow of your Leadership Talk. Most people tend to embrace the illusion of permanency rather than the reality of change. Be aware that the most passionate devotees of the status quo are often the very people who claim to have been motivated to take action for results. Not that they're deceiving you—they may be ardently committed to your leadership, but the psychological attractions of the status quo are sometimes irresistible. Be vigilant in perceiving those attractions. Be resolute in defeating them. The supervisor was struggling against an entrenched status quo. Answering this question helped her deflect the attack of that status quo and begin to change it. The status quo can only be changed through leadership that achieves more results, faster, continually.

Question 4: What does the audience feel?

On his first day on the job, the CEO of a struggling consumer products company fired the head of sales and marketing. The new sales and marketing leader showed me the tailspin sales numbers for the past three quarters.

She said, "What did Doctor Johnson say? 'If a man is going to be hanged in a fortnight, it concentrates the mind wonderfully.' I'm going to have a meeting with my direct reports and show them these numbers. They'll concentrate their minds."

"Watch out: the issue isn't just about the concentration of minds.

I'd bet their minds are concentrated already. The issue is what will they concentrate their minds *on*? Are they concentrated on what you want? That meeting might turn into a circular firing squad. Tell me, have you thought about their feelings?"

"Feelings, *schmeelings*! This isn't psychobabble-ology, Brent—this is business. We're in free fall. If their feelings get in the way of results—tough."

"I'm talking about results too. I'm talking about getting results from a Leadership Talk. The Leadership Talks is a results generator. It's meant not to simply help you get average results but get more results and faster results on a continual basis. Now, if your audience's feelings will help you generate those kinds of results, would they be important to you?"

"Whatever works. But I don't see how."

"Let's focus on what's happening. You're going to show them the numbers. That's O.K., but you're about to stumble into a trap many leaders get into. It prevents leaders from motivating others to lead their cause. The trap is misconstruing feelings for facts. Facts don't change, feelings do. Your feelings aren't facts; they're a response to facts. In this case, the numbers are the facts. You have your feelings about those facts; they have their feelings about those facts. And if you don't understand what their feelings are about those facts, you won't have much chance of motivating them to be your cause leaders. Are their feelings about those numbers different from yours?"

"How could they be? Numbers are numbers. We've got to turn them around. If their feelings are otherwise, they're in the wrong jobs!"

"Do they feel they're getting blamed for those numbers?"

"Nobody's blaming anybody."

"That's *your* reality. Is it *their* reality?"

"Their reality is what I tell them it is."

"That's right—if you're an order leader, you can surely order them to change those numbers. Order leadership gets results, and often gets more results faster. But does order leadership get more results faster, *continually*?"

"Probably not. I can't order them to get more and faster results continually. Ordering people might be a short-term solution, but it's not a long-term solution. If people could be ordered to hit big numbers continually, then the sales of every business would rocket off the charts. People have to make the choice to make it happen."

"Let's see if we can get a better idea of how their feelings link to results. Can we look at their feelings as a field?"

"What do you mean by 'field'?"

"In physics, a field is a region of space under the influence of some force, such as electricity or magnetism. In the same way, your audience's feelings can be a field—a region of your organization influenced by the force of their feelings."

"Your analogy may be a stretch, Brent, but I'll go with it. When you look at the feelings of everybody combined, yes, they could be construed as a kind of field."

"Are they a field of force?"

"That's one way to look at it. Their feelings are a field of force. At least, their feelings can create forceful actions."

"Then if the force field of their feelings can lead to powerful actions, would it behoove you to understand it?"

"Yes—if we're still talking about *continually.*"

"And must you do more than simply understand this force field?"

She laughed. "May the force be with you, Brent!"

"This isn't a fantasy. This is a reality check. Must you not only understand the force field, but also be able to use it, put it to work… that is, if *continually* is in the results equation?"

"Yes. But their feelings aren't necessarily a field that I'll accept. Results are. I'm not going to pander to their feelings to get results. Results can't be compromised for feelings."

"I agree. You need to get results, no excuses, and no compromises. I'm not talking about compromising your results, or about pandering to their feelings. Just the opposite, in fact, I'm talking about their feelings helping you get more results. Again, do your direct reports feel that they're getting blamed for the numbers?"

"They might feel that they're being made the scapegoats for bad decisions of the previous CEO and my predecessor."

"What do you think they'll feel about *you* showing them the numbers?"

"Upset. They might think I'm playing a blame game. But I don't care. Those numbers were generated on their watch. They're accountable."

"But isn't accountability not just what we accept but who we are?"

"Are you saying you don't want me to hurt their feelings?"

"No. I'm saying you must identify what you're dealing with. Then you have two choices."

"Let me see if I get it. Choice number one is that I have to convince them their feelings are irrelevant in terms of the results we have to get."

"Right. Is that an easy sell?"

"That's a tough sell."

"Why?"

"People's feelings are their very existence. I had a boss who said that my feelings on the job were irrelevant and to ignore them and just get the job done. I took his advice, but it got me angry because my feelings were me, and he was in essence saying I was irrelevant. You can't ignore your feelings. They're always there."

"That gets to choice number two."

"Which is tell them their feelings are relevant in terms of results. O.K., but where do I go from here?"

"What's the best thing you could do?"

"Make their feelings tools for results?"

"Right."

"But how?"

"By transforming their feelings into concrete, results-producing processes. I'll show you how later. Now, I want you to understand how important your audience's feelings are, not simply for their sake but for your sake, for the sake of results. I'm not saying you must agree with those feelings. Instead, understand their feelings so you're prepared to meet the challenges that flow from the forces that they create. If you don't, you're in a trap."

For a summary of how this Leadership Talk turned out, see Appendix B.

Lessons

Recognize that your audience's feelings are vital to your achieving results. This transcends simple awareness. Cultivate strong interest in those feelings. After all, why shouldn't you be interested in the feelings that are dearest to your audience—theirs? Initially, the executive wasn't interested. She saw their feelings as impediments to results. She didn't know that the real impediment was her bias. When she changed her mind, she began to position herself to give a Leadership Talk. There is, of course, a difference between being strongly interested in people's feelings and being nosy: the former evidences a concern for others, the latter a concern for yourself.

It's not necessary for you to precisely identify their feelings. Mind reading and Ouija board communication don't further the Leadership Talk. Often, your identification will be little more than a working hypothesis, but that hypothesis can lead to proof that helps achieve big rewards. A working hypothesis is a powerful leadership tool: it compels you to try to establish proof. The executive had to work out the proof of her don't-blame-me hypothesis by going out and interacting with her direct reports, probing their concerns, eliciting their advice. She eventually developed proof. Her direct reports did indeed feel that they were being unfairly blamed for the failures of the past. But since the labor of identification is often more useful than its fruits, she established with them a more open, honest, trusting, and productive relationship.

Focus on the vital feelings. Whether your audience is one person or many, they have myriad feelings. Take accurate aim by asking what they feel about the results they're expected to get Their feelings toward you are influenced by the expected results. If they feel that the results aren't worth the effort, they'll resent your trying to motivate them. The executive found out that her audience was eager to meet high expectations as long as they could take leadership in doing so.

Identify the objective causes of their feelings. Most feelings have objective causes. For instance, if your audience feels betrayed, try to comprehend the specific factors that *they* believe are at the root of that betrayal. In the executive's case, the audience was convinced that the previous CEO and sales-and-marketing chief were relentless micro-managers who refused to allow anyone to make even minor decisions and insisted that their wrongheaded ideas be carried out, no questions asked. The direct reports were convinced that they were taking the fall for the other guys. Regarding the Leadership Talk, seeing isn't believing—believing is also seeing. When they understood that their leadership (not their robotic follower-ship) was going to be the new order of the day, their feelings no longer obstructed results but launched them.

Question 5: What does the audience fear?

Since fear is the cocaine of leadership, powerful in its immediate effects but destructive in the long run, how do we understand how it fits in with the Leadership Talk? First, let's understand that fear comes with most quests for results. In fact, if we lack a measure of fear concerning an undertaking, it's usually not important enough to undertake. So, the challenge of fear isn't its elimination, but dealing with and ultimately using fear.

A financial leader of a company whose revenues had slowed told me, "Our financial operations have to wring out more efficiencies. If we don't, how can I expect the other functions to do it?"

"How do they view your operations?"

"As the company's traffic cops."

"How do you want to be viewed?"

"As their results partners."

"Where does that change in point of view have to start?"

"With us. We have to change ours before we can have them change theirs. The efficiencies crusade is the way to make that change happen. The trouble is, I can't get my financial people to sign on to the crusade."

"Why?"

"They're interested—but not motivated."

"What do you mean?"

"They're interested because I'm their boss and I'm saying it, but they're not motivated because they have financial projects coming out of their ears. They simply don't have the time for another project, let alone a crusade."

"A crusade is a crusade. Can't you make it *the* top priority?"

"All our projects are top priority."

"Do you want my diagnosis?"

"Be the doctor."

"If you can't motivate people to take the action you want, heal thyself, leader."

"Go on."

"You don't have a worker problem, you have a leadership problem."

"What's the problem?"

"Your inability to get them to sign on to the crusade."

"My inability? Their *unwillingness* is the problem."

"Your inability has created their unwillingness."

"What's the treatment?"

"A pill. It's called the Leadership Talk—a bunch of them every day."

"Where do I start?"

"By reminding yourself what the fundamental function of a Leadership Talk is—and that's to get a cause leader or cause leaders who'll help achieve more results, faster, on a continual basis. That never changes. You can give a thousand Leadership Talks, and that function will always be the same."

"But I can't wave a magic wand and *poof!*—they're cause leaders."

"The Leadership Talk isn't magic, but process. Let's work the process. Have you answered the question 'What do they fear?'"

"Sure. They fear botching up their work if they get overloaded."

"Yes, that's a fear, an important fear. But is it the most important fear?"

"There's a more important fear?"

"What's the root fear?"

"Losing their jobs."

"Does that apply here?"

"No."

"Why?"

"They've got job security."

"In writing?"

"Of course not. The security is growth. This is a growing business. They're badly needed."

"Who says so?"

"Me. The CEO. The business itself."

"Your growth has slowed down."

"Hence the crusade."

"What will happen if the crusade succeeds?"

"We'll be more efficient, more productive. We'll create a lot more output with a lot less input."

"'Less' meaning jobs?"

"Maybe. If we're cutting resources, we might be cutting jobs—or at least changing job descriptions."

"Haven't you just answered the question 'What do they fear?'"

"They fear job loss? But, Brent, the problem I have with what you're saying is, I can't be sure what they fear until I ask them."

"Yes, and when you ask them, they themselves might not know what they fear. They might not even know that they fear. Or if they do know, they might not want to tell you."

"Exactly. So why even ask the question?"

"Let me answer that with a couple of analogies. When a surgeon goes to operate, the surgeon might not know precisely what he or she will find inside the patient's body; but doesn't the surgeon have a good idea of what's there?"

"Sure, the surgeon's training, knowledge, and skills are focused on understanding where organs are, their function, and their interactions."

"Doesn't that foreknowledge better prepare the surgeon to deal with both the expected and the unexpected?"

"Of course."

"And if you begin a voyage, isn't it better to have a good idea of the weather and the seas and the hazards you'll encounter, though you might not know precisely what they'll be?"

"Of course."

"Then in the case of the Eight Questions, isn't it better to ask them, even if you don't have precise answers?"

"Yes. Asking without knowing can help prepare me to deal better with my audience. You might say that the questions—or asking the questions—can often be more important than the answers you get."

"Yes. Now, let's go back to your challenge. You've got an audience that's interested but not motivated. You need to move them out of simply being interested and into the realm of being motivated to take action that achieves more results, faster, continually. One way is to ask what they fear, and use their answers as tools for results."

"Okay."

"Farmers have a saying, 'You can't get a hog to butcher itself.' Might that apply here?"

"It might. So what?"

"The answer to that is a solution to your problem. Is your problem a skill issue or a will issue?"

"A will issue, for the most part."

"If it were a skill issue, what would you do?"

"Simple. Get them trained or get them out and get somebody else who has the skills."

"But since it's a will issue, what do you do?"

"I don't know."

"But you *do* know. You just told me you know what to do—and you don't know that you told me. You don't know that you have the answer."

He laughed, "Butcher the hog myself?"

"You said you can't be sure what they fear. But when you really analyze the situation, isn't it pretty obvious what they fear? The hog sees butchered hogs; the hog sees the knife."

"O.K., maybe I get it. When you and I first started talking, I thought their reluctance was linked to job performance, but now I see that it might be linked to job security—though, of course, I really can't be sure until I talk with them."

"If job security, not job performance, is their root problem, what must you do?"

"Clearly, I have to do *something*. They won't become my cause leaders until I do something about their fear that their job security is threatened—if that's what they really fear."

"Later, we'll decide what you might do, which will involve finding the problem or problems in the fear, and then challenging your audience to take leadership to identify and effect the solutions. For now, it's enough that you know there's something to do. People often want to jump right in and tackle the problems of the needs in the needs stage. But I tell them to hold off until they come to grips with the belief and action stages. At the needs stage, we're simply identifying and validating their needs. Just doing that is crucial. Getting the right need, the root need, clearly identified, and then getting their agreement that it's the right need, is a great start in developing Leadership Talks."

"O.K., I see now that they might fear that the efficiencies they create won't jeopardize just the way they do their jobs, but maybe the jobs themselves. And if I don't do something about that fear, I don't have cause leaders, and the crusade is dead."

For a summary of how this Leadership Talk turned out, see Appendix B.

Lessons

Understand that most of the leadership challenges you face are defined by some degree of fear, small or large. Every fear has value and purpose. Fear isn't to be rejected or avoided, but faced, understood—and used.

Identify the precise causes of your audience's fear (and your own), and you have powerful material for a Leadership Talk. For instance, a common fear is fear of failure. You might ask your audience to identify precisely what problems will cause them to fail, and then challenge them to take leadership action to solve those problems.

If people can't feel it, they won't lead it. Because of their fears, the financial leader's audience couldn't feel the necessity for the financial crusade. He was wasting his time on the crusade—until he tackled the challenges of those fears, which centered on job security, not just job performance.

Fear is both stimulant and depressant. It can motivate people to do extraordinary things. Yet, if it becomes embedded in an organization, people get depressed, get embittered, and often get out.

Their average solutions to the problems of their fears are often far better than your supposedly great solutions. So, your best Leadership Talk might not come from you, but from them, as they talk about their leadership for solutions.

Question 6: What's the Major Problem of the Audience?

People have many problems, but when you understand their most important problem, you're ready to give a Leadership Talk. Here's an example: A CEO asked me to help with a series of presentations he planned to give to his lieutenants.

He said, "Signing on to this company might've been the biggest mistake of my life."

"Why?"

"The CEO I replaced was the founder of the company, a star of the industry, and a beloved patriarch. He retired in a cloud of rising profits and a hearty 'Hi-ho Silver.' This Lone Ranger's last words on the podium at the retirement gala, just after he got a standing O, were, 'Don't screw up the business!' I was at the gala. When I heard those parting words, I wanted to make a career U-turn and get back to my old company. A long time ago, my father said to me, 'Never replace the star of an organization—you'll never last. Instead, replace the person who replaced the star.' I forgot about that advice until now. Well, here I am, so I'm going to start off by giving presentations on the state of the business and how we can do better."

"Hold on," I said. "Why presentations? Why not give Leadership Talks instead?"

"O.K., why?"

"Is there a difference between the two?"

"A crucial difference, Brent. Presentations provide information. Leadership Talks get people motivated and moving."

"As a general rule, should most communications be presentations or Leadership Talks?"

"As a rule, Leadership Talks."

"The saying, 'You never get a second chance to make a first impression' applies here. More than that, you've got a great opportunity to get them moving in the right way, in the right direction. Let me ask you, what's the major problem of your leaders?"

"Who knows? I could think of a lot of problems they have. If you asked each of them, you'd probably come up with a different problem for every individual."

"Of course. But the purpose of this question isn't to discern every major problem of each individual in your audience. This isn't psycho-analysis. The question's objective is to help you identify and understand a results-producing dynamic."

"If my asking and answering that question helps me get more results, it's damned important. Otherwise, forget it. But you haven't convinced me that it is."

"And if you're not convinced that the question is important, then the answers are useless."

"I'm convinced of that!"

"First, results come in many forms, but they have only one fundamental substance. To know that substance, you don't go to results themselves, but to the people who must get the results. Let's be clear about the reason for the question. When people get together, do their needs change?"

"The way I look at it, everybody pretty much has the same general needs: the need to succeed, to be liked, to be understood, and so on. But when people get together in groups, different needs may be highlighted. For example, when I get together with my son's Little League committee, I might be rushed for time and can't spend more than an hour in the meeting. If it goes well past the hour, I'm going to have a growing need to get out of there."

"So, if your needs change, or at least become subject to different highlights, as you said, do the needs of all individuals who come together in a group become highlighted in different ways?"

"In most cases."

"And would the changes in highlights be linked to the challenges of the group?"

"Yes."

"And would some needs or problems, as they relate to the challenges of the group, be perceived as more important than other needs?"

"Yes."

"And because there may be a rough priority in the perceived importance of needs/problems, might there be one that's the major problem?"

"You changed needs into problems."

"For the purposes of the Leadership Talk, don't you think that needs and problems are the same thing? If you have a need, isn't that a problem looking for a solution?"

"Yes."

"Given a rough priority of needs/problems, might there be a major one?"

"Not necessarily. Different members of the group might perceive the group as having different problems. You probably have a spectrum of major problems."

"Might there be a single major problem that most, if not all, members of the group agree on?"

"In some cases, yes, in others, no. You might have an audience that's polarized."

"That's a special case. If you have an audience that is polarized on issues, you have to bridge the poles before you can identify a single major problem." See the lessons for an explanation on how to bridge the poles.

"Should we then have an idea of that single major problem, the one that manifested because they've gotten together as a group—that group problem, if you will—if we want to have the members of that group get moving?"

"That's the key issue here. What does our understanding of their single major problem have to do with getting them moving?"

"What will they think of you if they perceive that you don't know or care what their major problem is?"

"They'd probably get angry."

"Why?"

"Brent, remember the saying, 'People won't care that you know unless they know that you care.' Their problem is their reality. And being in a particular group, their reality might be their problem. If they think I don't know about or care about their reality, I myself have a major problem, which is that *I* have become their problem. And if they see me as their problem, they'll march to the beat of another drummer, certainly not mine."

"So you've answered your question about the importance of this question."

"O.K., you've convinced me."

"No, you convinced yourself. You had the answer, not me. Let's find out the single major problem of the people you'll be talking to, and see if we can apply it to help you get results."

"But why this focus on the single major problem? Why not a lot of major problems? Why not most of their major problems?"

"The verb you used answered your own question."

"Focus?"

"Is focus important?"

"In leadership, in communication, focus is indispensable."

"So, does coming to understand their single major problem help provide focus?"

"I see. Not precise but approximate focus. I'm beginning to understand that much of the power of a Leadership Talk comes from approximations. It's not science, but art."

"The Leadership Talk isn't all art; there's some science involved in it too. But right now, let's apply the art. Let's find out your audience's major problem."

"To find out, we can only ask them when they get together."

"Not necessarily. We can also ask them separately first. We can at least then get a working hypothesis. Remember the power of approximations."

"Brent, from one ex-Marine to another, why don't you do a little recon?"

Off I went to talk with a few of the lieutenants. In my talks, a single need kept cropping up. When I conveyed it to the new CEO, he was surprised.

"Lack of confidence? In *me*?"

"No, in themselves."

"Where'd you pull that one out of, left field?"

"Does it make sense?"

"No. This is a successful business."

"Sometimes the cruelest price of leadership is success. Let's look at your predecessor."

"Well, he pretty much ran the business himself. His leaders could act only after they got clearance from him."

"That's being indispensable?"

"I thought that was a compliment. Now I see it the other way around. He developed the business, but he didn't develop his leaders. My challenge is to do both."

For a summary of how this Leadership Talk turned out, see Appendix B.

Lessons

Every group of people to whom you give Leadership Talks has a major problem. That problem usually stems from the reasons why they've gathered together. When you identify their major problem, you've revealed important information for your Talk.

You might find out that their major problem isn't related to the problem that you as a leader are facing. But before you can elicit their cause leadership in solving your problem, you first must understand and respect theirs.

There are three ways to identify their major problem:

1. **Extrapolate what it is from your assessment of their situation.**
2. **Ask them outright.**
3. **Combine the first two.**

You don't necessarily have to understand their major problem in full detail before you begin to address it. We ask for precision in identifying the audience's major problem only insofar as the subject admits of it. We're not looking for mathematical rigor, but general guidelines that will help us help them make the choice to be our cause leaders.

Understand the links between their major problem and why you're there. That linkage contains the value that they perceive you bring to them. When they see that you offer solutions to their problem, you're better positioned to win them over to be your cause leaders. However, if they see that you offer no solutions, or are even an impediment to solutions, you may become the audience's major problem, with little chance of gaining such commitment from them.

When developing a solution to their major problem, you can start finding the solution in the answers to the Eight Needs Questions. Audiences usually have the solutions to their problems, but can't see those solutions in the fog of their emotions or the confusion of the situation. Your identification of their emotions and analysis of their situation can point to ways that will help them come to their own rescue.

Trust is a key element of your using the major problem for good effect in the Leadership Talk. If they don't trust you, they'll probably conceal their major problem from you. If they don't trust you, they'll be suspicious of your helping them find a solution. If they don't trust you, they'll likely reject your challenge to be cause leaders.

Often you'll want to give a Leadership Talk to an audience whose members comprise opposite poles of an issue. In that case, it's best to address each single major problem of the opposing audience segments. Then discuss what bridges those poles. Do that by raising the stakes. Let's say that one part of the audience wants to go right and the other part wants to go left. You talk to one part of the audience about going right, then talk to the other part about going left. Finally, raise the stakes. Talk about how disastrous—or necessary—wanting to go in opposite directions is to your overall goals. Develop a common, overriding goal that they both can march toward.

Is there a difference between what you think is their major problem and what they think it is? They cannot be motivated to be your cause leaders unless you both reconcile that difference.

Question 7: What makes the audience angry?

An operations leader told me, "I'm convinced: more results, faster, on a continual basis is the way to go. It's all about controlling one's destiny before somebody else does. So I'm instituting a culture of more results, faster, continually, throughout operations."

"How?" I asked.

He said, "The employees of each function that report to me are identifying and accomplishing specific actions toward that end. But here's the problem: we've streamlined our organization, so the logistics and administrative departments report to me too. I'm told that many of the employees in those functions are angry about the initiative."

"Who told you this?"

"Not the function heads. Roundabout sources told me. I think the administration and logistics chiefs are reluctant to bring that issue to me."

"If the reports are accurate, you're suffering from the Leader's Fallacy."

"What's that?"

"The belief that your enthusiasm is automatically reciprocated. Don't you think that often an inverse equation operates?"

"Yes. I've found out that what excites leaders often angers the people they're leading. Over my career, I've seen efforts like increased productivity, enhanced customer service, reduced cycle time, et cetera, anger the people who are supposed to carry them out."

"Leaders cast a lot of seeds among thorns."

"It sounds very Biblical, Brent. But what do I do about it?"

"First, you have to decide if their anger's acceptable or not."

"Clearly, it's not. There's no way I'm going to institute a culture of more results faster leading angry people. A house divided against itself can't get more results, faster, continually. I need everybody's full commitment. Angry people are committed first and foremost to their anger and the actions they take caused by that anger."

"Then what's the next step?"

"Obviously, to do something about it. I have to find out what makes them angry."

"Yes. Most leaders don't know that the people they're trying to motivate are angry. Even if they do know, they don't care that they're angry, and even if they care, they don't know what to do about it. The fact that you know gives you great advantage. You not only know what's making them angry, but also what to do about it. If you didn't, you either haven't been their leader long or you're OTTO—oblivious to the obvious. Good leaders are MOTO—masters of the obvious. They see more obvious things than poor leaders do. What's the obvious in this situation?"

"They see themselves as second-class citizens within the company."

"Why?"

"Sales and marketing, production—those functions get the attention and recognition from senior management. They get the bulk of the resources. So the logistics and administrative people think that more-results-faster initiatives are for the so-called glory functions. Also, they're angry about having to participate in something they believe interferes with their daily jobs."

"So they have double reason to be angry?"

"Now that I think of it, yes. People who define themselves as second-class citizens usually get angry when they're forced to serve the so-called first-class citizens."

"What's the obvious solution?"

"Well, you always say, Brent, that every strong emotion is a problem looking for a solution. So, I should provide solutions to that problem."

"Really?"

"Let me rephrase that. *They* should provide solutions to their problem. It's like teaching a person to fish instead of handing out fish."

"Oh?"

"I'll rephrase that too. It's like teaching that person to take *leadership* of fishing."

"And where does that begin?"

"With their emotion and the problem in the emotion."

"What's their emotional reality?"

"Their anger. We have to start with their anger. They have to recognize that they're angry. That's not as easy as it sounds. I've found that angry people often don't want to face the fact that they're angry. Next, they have to tell me that they're angry. We have to get their anger out on the table."

"Why?"

"If they keep it to themselves and don't convey it to me, it'll fester, and we're back to their being more committed to the festering anger than more results, faster, continually."

"And then?"

"And then recognize that it's their choice to do something about it."

"And then?"

"Develop precise actions to do something about it."

"What actions?"

"Leadership actions."

"When they're solving the problems of their anger, and I'm giving them the support to solve those problems, then they'll more likely be on board with my initiatives. And I've got to keep their leaders in the loop to prevent *their* getting angry."

For a summary of how this Leadership Talk turned out, see Appendix B.

Lessons

Anger and fear can be the defining emotions in nearly all of your leadership challenges. I said that fear is embodied in most leadership situations. Let's add anger to that mix. Anger and fear are deeply connected. We can understand the connection when we view the pharmacology of the two emotions. Hormonal excretions of our adrenal glands trigger our fears. Add just one atom to the molecule and fear becomes anger. Angry people are fearful—fearful people angry.

Don't dismiss anger out of hand. It's actually a kindness when it furthers results. When the people you lead are angry, ask, "Is their anger a help or a hindrance to results?" If the former, find ways to have them channel their anger into focused analysis and action. If the latter, go through the process of seeing that anger as a problem to which you challenge them to provide solutions. However, even positive anger, like positive fear, eventually wears out its welcome. An organization of angry people may get more results faster—but can it do it *continually*?

You can derive powerful material for a Leadership Talk by flipping the answers to the anger question and then providing a process to solve the problem of the flip side. For example, if your audience, like the audience of the operations leader, is angry that their worth on the job isn't being recognized, flip it: have them develop a strategy, resource stream, actions, and evaluation systems to have that worth recognized.

People who have low expectations of themselves are usually angry with themselves and their leaders. Eliminate the anger by raising their expectations. Raise expectations by:

1. Having them acknowledge that they have low expectations.
2. Getting their commitment to change those expectations.
3. Describing the best practices to show them how to raise those expectations.
4. Translating those practices to their jobs.
5. Providing specific milestones to measure their progress.
7. People get angry when:
   • their time is being wasted;
   • their individual worth isn't respected;

- they feel threatened;
- their efforts aren't appreciated;
- they're not given voice or choice in their work;
- their values aren't recognized or given credence;
- their leaders can't do their jobs well;
- their leaders focus on their own needs;
- their leaders don't understand and acknowledge their needs
- their leaders don't provide clear direction.

Question 8: What do they dream?

A manager of a telecommunications company that had recently eliminated 11 percent of its workforce said, "Brent, I used to have one department reporting to me, but now I have three, all much reduced in size. They're angry. They're fearful. They're practically paralyzed. They seldom talk with one another, let alone with me. They're afraid to make decisions. They're just focused on wanting to be left alone to do their jobs. And that's the trouble. They do their jobs. They just *do* their jobs. They need to understand that just *doing* won't cut it. If our company's going to survive in this market, we have to be enterprising. We have to hustle just to stay even. We're being asked to do more with less; pretty soon we'll be asked to do everything with nothing. And if we don't, there'll be even bigger cuts down the road."

"What do they dream?"

He said, "Whoa! Where'd that come from? What do dreams have to do with it?"

"Maybe nothing. Maybe everything."

"How the hell should I know what they dream? Or *care* what they dream? Brent, we don't turn out the lights and speak to the dead. I'm talking about practical reality here."

"So am I."

"What's practical about dreams?"

"The action that they trigger."

"I'll bite. Go on."

"Let's first look at what dreams are all about in an organization. Can dreams be powerful motivators?"

"Yes. Hey, I once dreamed that I'd play center field for the New York Yankees. That dream was a powerful motivator. Playing baseball was my passion for years. I skipped college to go into the minor leagues. But then I found out that I didn't have it to play center field for the Class-D Pittsfield Mets, let alone the Yankees."

"Your dream was reality?"

"It was in my imagination, of course—but it caused me to take real action."

"So dreams can lead to action?"

"I'll go even further. I'll say that dreams have their life in action. The reality of my dream was in my passion for playing."

"Then let's look at the people in your departments. If you say that dreams influence—"

"More than influence, they *live* in action."

"So, if dreams live in actions, might not the dreams of the people in your department be important?"

"Yes. If they relate to the actions people take on their jobs. A big *if.*"

"What's their reaction to the job cuts?"

"Obviously, they're traumatized. Their good friends have gotten their walking papers. They've seen their departments undergo drastic changes. Their world has been turned upside down."

"In this environment of turmoil, do they dream?"

"They probably dream of better days."

"Better days in the future or the past?"

"Our future is uncertain. We might lose our jobs in the future. The past is what they know, so they're probably dreaming of the old days."

"The old days before the cuts?"

"Yes. Come to think of it, that's a refrain I've heard a lot from many of them. They wish they were back in the good old days before the cuts, when they're friends were still here, and no one had to worry about job security."

"Haven't you just described a powerful dream of theirs?"

"The dream of going back to the good old days? I guess. But so what?"

"You've just stumbled on the key to turning the departments around. Why might their dream be the key to your success? The answer goes back to you and the New York Yankees."

"Back then, as long as I thought that I had a chance to realize my dream, I worked my tail off. But once I understood that there was no way, I had to make a choice: I had to choose to continue dreaming an impossible dream or find a new dream.

"So you needed to have a dream of some kind?"

"I haven't thought about it this way, but I believe everybody needs to dream; more than that, everybody has a dream, whether they know it or not."

"Including the employees reporting to you now?"

"Including them."

"So, you've just described the key that you stumbled on."

"Let me take a shot at it. The employees have a dream, the good-old-days dream. Like me back in my baseball days, they have to decide if it's an attainable dream. Clearly, it's not. As long as they're driven by that dream, they won't give their best to their work. It's a toxic dream. They must dream a dream that's positive in terms of their actions on the job, and that will help them do their best."

"Are you talking about changing their dream?"

"I guess I am. They have to find a new dream. But how?"

"First, whose choice is it to find a new dream?"

"It's their choice, not mine. How do I help them make the choice to dream a new dream?"

"There's only one way—the new dream has to embody a solution."

"When their new dream is a solution to a major problem of theirs? Now I see. My major problem, after I realized the Yankees weren't in my future, was deciding what to do with the rest of my life."

"What's their major problem?"

"Job security. They feel as if they're walking around with expiration dates printed on their foreheads."

"Does the good-old-days dream help them get job security?"

"Of course not. In fact, it prevents them from throwing themselves wholeheartedly into their present jobs—which might even screw up what little job security they have—if they have any at all, which they—we—probably don't. Just as I had to consciously realize how my dream of being a baseball player was affecting my life, they must realize what their good-old-days dream is doing to their job performance. That's my job—to talk to them about it, have them come to that realization, and then have them make the choice to change or not change. Those who choose to change can move forward with me; those who choose not to change, who still want to cling to the good-old-days dream, they and I have some work to do together."

"So what have you learned in our discussion?"

"Dreams are action. Great results must be grounded in positive dreams. And lousy results can be grounded in toxic dreams."

For a summary of how this Leadership Talk turned out, see Appendix B.

Lessons

Dreams are not only action, but also give meaning to action. People dreaming, for instance, of wanting to go back to the good old days will be committed to actions that help further such a dream, and will resent having to act against it. The best of organizations seldom prevail against a toxic dream.

Look at the dreams of the people you lead as being practical, concrete functions. The good-old-days dreams of the people in the manager's departments had functional results.

People who believe they're living their dream see work as a higher cause to which they are summoned, and usually will try to motivate others to join them in that cause.

Every dream has a value for the dreamer. Does the individual's dream have value for the organization? If so, the organization must celebrate and support that dream. If not, you as a leader must have the dreamer make the choice to change the dream.

If you don't believe in their dream, they won't believe in you. If they have a dream that you can't believe in, you must help them change that dream.

A dream is often the flip side of a fear. The employees feared that they'd eventually lose their jobs. Their good-old-days dream was particularly toxic because it motivated them to deal with that fear in the wrong ways.

Business-related dreams may be different from home-related dreams. If their business-related dream conflicts with the home-related dream, you might have a toxic dream percolating. For instance, you might be asking them to take on more work to meet an unexpected opportunity, but they might not be spending the time they want with their families. Result: they dream of getting another job. When motivating them to get results, take into account both their home and their work dreams. Understand precisely what their work and home dreams are and the relative importance of each. Integrate those dreams. Clashing dreams of work and home discourage the dreamers. Resonating dreams of work and home (i.e., dreams that reinforce and enrich each other) encourage and motivate dreamers.

Recap of the Eight Questions

The Eight Questions are the navigation system of the Leadership Talk. They show you the psychological terrain you're dealing with when you intend to have others sign up to be your cause leaders, and guide you through that terrain. Don't be discouraged by the number of questions and by the fact that at first you might feel awkward using them. As you put the questions to constant use, you'll find that they become integrated into your mental processes.

Psychologists observe that there are roughly four stages of advancement when one undertakes to learn new skills: unconscious incompetence; conscious incompetence; conscious competence; unconscious competence. This applies to the Eight Questions as well. As you continually use them, you'll see that it takes less and less time to think them through in a conscious way. The questions become most powerful as tools of the Leadership Talk when you're working them at the unconscious competence level, asking and answering them almost instantly.

Practice

Phase 1: First, simply become aware of people's needs. Observe people at work, in your family, and your social network. Understand them in terms of their needs. See how their needs and emotions are interrelated. Watch how those needs change, and watch what remains the same. See what needs impel them to take action. Let your interest grow naturally out of your observations. A plant manager in a utilities company told me that an important element of his success using Leadership Talks stems from the gradual way he introduced them into his working environment. "After coming back from your seminar, Brent, I gave no Leadership Talks for nearly two weeks. People had their eyes on me. They were waiting for me to come back and make changes. But I made none. I simply observed people and their needs. Then, gradually, unobtrusively, I began giving Leadership Talks. Now, a year and a half later, I give them all the time. My leaders give them all the time. Those Talks have flowed organically out of our daily situations, and have led to increased results. The Leadership Talk is one of the best things that's happened to us, but it might not have happened if I had introduced it prematurely."

Phase 2: After becoming generally aware of the needs of your potential cause leaders, begin making specific identifications. Talk with them about their needs. Be rigorous in your analysis. Come to an agreement with them as to precisely what those needs are. In most cases, your first identification is superficial. Keep digging until you get to the root needs. In many cases, people aren't consciously aware of their needs. Helping them become aware helps you give strong Leadership Talks.

Phase 3: Move from identification and analysis to interaction. Start injecting people's needs into your written and verbal interactions with them. Don't tell people what their needs are. Get into the mode of asking them. As you progress, you'll find that the question mark is one of the most effective tools of the Leadership Talk. It's far better if they tell you than if you tell them. Start talking about needs as ways to get results. See the problems in the needs. Come to an agreement with them as to what those problems are. Challenge them to take leadership to solve those problems.

Now that you've become acquainted with the needs questions, we can move into the second trigger of the Three-Trigger Motivational process—belief.

Belief

Do you believe deeply in what you say? If you don't, the people you say it to are less likely to believe in you, let alone what they do for you. However, though your belief is necessary in persuading people to choose to be your cause leader, it's not sufficient. After all, most leaders are motivated; if you're not, you probably won't be a leader for long. The issue in the Leadership Talk is, how do you transfer your belief to them, how do you have your belief become their belief? I call it the Motivational Transfer. Without it, you can't consistently get cause leaders.

An automotive manufacturing head told me, "We're undergoing a company-wide restructuring. It's one of the biggest in the company's history. I'm on the steering committee and I have to give one of the initial talks describing the restructuring to a gathering of five hundred key leaders from all over the world. I agree about the dangers of my being a messenger in that situation. I'm not there simply to give them information."

"What *are* you there for?" I asked.

"Maybe that's my problem—honestly, I'm not quite sure. This is a critical situation. I have to clearly understand why I'm there speaking to them. If I don't, they sure won't. I know I'm expected to give a speech outlining the broad aspects of the restructuring, but I feel I should be doing something more."

"You're right. You should be. One way to look at what you should be doing is to ask, 'Should I give a presentation or a Leadership Talk?'"

"There are presentation aspects to what I'll be saying. I have to give an overview of the restructuring. And that will entail conveying specific information. But having said that, I need for my address to be something more. And that something more should be a Leadership Talk."

"When you're unsure about what your role is and what you're going to say, first be clear about what a Leadership Talk is. Be clearly conscious of it by stating the precise words—even if you've stated them before many times. It'll help you focus in the right way."

"Okay. A Leadership Talk is about one thing only: to get a cause leader or cause leaders."

"You can't stop there. Getting cause leaders isn't enough. Simply having cause leaders is fruitless unless—"

"Unless they're getting more results, faster, continually."

"So the function of every Leadership Talk is to get cause leaders who are aiming to achieve such results. Given that, what's your role?"

"Get cause leaders for the restructuring, get people leading, not simply doing. There's a big difference between these leaders *leading* the restructuring and simply doing it. It could be the difference between success and failure. What I say in my time slot might not have the audience sign up then and there to be cause leaders, but maybe I can at least get them well disposed toward the idea."

"How?"

"By having them begin to believe as deeply as I do about the restructuring. This is a big challenge. I'm excited about it and can't wait to get going on making it happen. When my excitement becomes theirs—when they can't wait to make these changes—I'll have delivered my message."

"So, aren't you starting to clarify your role?"

"My role is to have them begin to understand the restructuring, begin to believe in it, and then begin to see themselves as the leaders of it.

"Will they take this leadership if they lack your deep belief?"

"No. To take leadership in this, they have to share my beliefs."

"So, isn't a vital aspect of your role and your Leadership Talk the transference of your beliefs to them?"

"Of course."

"We're talking about the motivational transfer—one of the most important aspects of the Leadership Talk."

"But how do we do it?"

"There are three transfer agents: information, logic, and experience."

"I understand the first way. After all, when we're given new information, we often change our attitudes and behavior. Many smokers probably try to quit because of grim medical statistics. Look at my situation: my audience needs me to give them information about restructuring. When they get it, some of them might start believing as strongly as I do that it must happen. For example, we've been operating internationally, but we haven't been a truly global company. If we're going to compete against the Toyotas of the world, we can't have a worldwide manufacturing operation divided by fiefdoms. Instead, it has to be open to the world inside our company and the world outside, too. Those are just words, but I have facts to back them up, and those facts should help get at least some cause leaders. That's doing it by conveying information. But logic and experience—you'll have to explain those."

"Let's look at logic. Is motivation an emotional dynamic?"

"Yes."

"Does emotion have its roots in logic?"

"I'll have to think about that."

"I often use the 'crying policeman' as a thought experiment to analyze the hypothesis. Picture a policeman weeping, hair disheveled, coat unbuttoned, hands covering his face. Isn't it true that we don't know what to feel about that policeman until we can logically understand why he's weeping? He might be a homicidal manic who's been shooting at people, has run out of ammunition, and is acting out some crazed temper tantrum. Or, he might be a policeman who has spent all night trying to talk a man out of jumping off a bridge to his death, but the man jumped and the policeman is crying over the tragedy."

"I see. How we feel about the policeman runs along the tracks of logic. Logic helps make the motivational transfer happen. Unless people can logically understand the reality that's facing them, they'll be confused about what to feel about that reality. And confusion rarely gets you a cause leader."

"How does that relate to your transferring your belief about the restructuring?"

"Unless it makes sense to them, I'll be doing all the believing and they'll be doing none of it. So I have to make sure the information I present is as logical as a lag bolt. O.K., we've got information and logic. But what about experience?"

"Experience can be the most powerful transfer agent of the three, yet most leaders either ignore it or are afraid to get near it. Let's go back to the basics of motivational transfer. In terms of the Leadership Talk, does motivation happen when you alone are motivated?"

"No, only when your belief becomes their belief. Information and logic help transfer belief. I see that, but I'm looking forward to seeing how experience is the ace card."

"Generally speaking, humans learn in two ways: through intellectual understanding and through experience. Agree?"

"In a general sense, yes—though I'm a little uncomfortable about where this is going. After all, I have a major communication to make. I don't have the time or the inclination to indulge in Education 101."

"But haven't you said that you need to know your role in this situation?"

"Yes."

"So what I'm going to say has everything to do with that role and what your audience perceives it to be. When you stand up to talk to your audience, you're going to be directed in part by assumptions that you make about your role. The words you use, the position you hold, your being on the steering committee, the CEO's trust in you, the integrity you're known for, your inflection, even the clothes you wear… all these things and many more drive assumptions you make about yourself in the moment you stand before them—and the assumptions they make about you."

"O.K., all those assumptions shape my relationships with them—relationships that will decide the success or failure of my Leadership Talk."

"Are those assumptions learned?"

"Of course."

"Did that learning come from intellectual understanding or experience?"

"Both. But without the knowledge that came from experience, the assumptions would have little meaning. We may acquire intellectual knowledge, but for that knowledge to be an important factor in our lives, it must be given value through the test of experience."

"Now let's apply that principle to your situation. You said you feel strongly that the restructuring has to take place. Let's look at where that strong belief comes from. If you don't know its roots, then you can't transfer it to your audience."

"We've been running after Toyota for years in terms of quality, productivity, and manufacturing efficiencies. We've improved a lot, but we haven't closed the gap. They've improved too. We're not moving ahead fast enough to overtake them. We're not losing ground anymore, but we're not gaining much ground either. We need to make a quantum leap. This restructuring will help us do it."

"That's information. It's good, logical information, and it must be communicated to your audience. But you haven't gone far enough. You haven't put in your experience. Until you do, your Leadership Talk won't be as powerful as it can be. In fact, until you do, you have more of a presentation than a Leadership Talk."

"What experience, Brent? What are you talking about?"

"Why close the gap? Why not settle for second best?"

"There are a lot of answers: stock price, jobs, growth, careers."

"But what about you personally?"

"Personally? I can tell you about 'personally.' My father owned our company's tractor dealership in the town I grew up in. Those were the best tractors built. The company was number one. I grew up with that feeling in my bones."

"So, to have your company settle for second best—"

"That's unacceptable. You talk about where my strong feelings come from. That's where they come from."

"So, if you can transfer those powerful feelings to your audience, what will that do for your Leadership Talk?"

"It'll put it on a much higher plane. It'll make it more than a simple communication of information. It'll make it an experience for the audience. But you're setting a pretty high standard here. This is a business environment. We're not talking about a religious epiphany."

"Let's leave out the word "religious" and keep the word "epiphany." An epiphany is an irresistibly strong experience. Hasn't your career been full of such experiences?"

"Of course."

"Is business devoid of such experiences?"

"Business *is* such experiences."

"Does your speaking challenge call for the audience to have a strong experience?"

"Yes. They can't just take action. For the restructuring to really work, they have to really want to take action, and not just any kind of action—it has to be leadership action. They won't really want to unless they first have a strong experience listening to me and the other leaders speaking that day."

"So the issue is, how does your really wanting to become their really wanting to?"

"O.K., now I agree. But how are we going to do it?"

"Through the motivational transfer process. We can't make the motivational transfer now and then, hit or miss. We must do it consistently. It's self-evident how we communicate information and provide structure. But when it comes to transferring our experience to them so that it becomes their experience, we need a process. Process provides precision, power, and consistency."

"Process, I understand. When you combine motivation with it, you get me a little confused."

"Here's the process, and you can use it for every Leadership Talk you give. It's simple and it works. The first step is that you have to understand the vital importance of transferring your experience. You have to believe it must be done and can be done."

"I do now."

"The second step is to examine your strong emotion. You said that it stemmed from your childhood and your father owning the tractor franchise."

"Yes."

"The third step is to recollect a strong, emotional experience, a defining moment, related to that. Remember where you were at the time. Remember what physical action was taking place."

"I just remember walking up to the dealership. I did it many times, but it almost seems like they're all rolled into one time. I'm walking up and seeing the tractors and my father talking with people, and just feeling a tremendous pride that I'm somehow part of the very best in the world."

"That's what you describe to your audience."

"But that's a personal experience, Brent. What's it got to do with a global restructuring?"

"Here's a fundamental principle of the motivational transfer. When a leader talks, an audience asks two questions, whether they're conscious of asking them or not. The first is, 'Can you do your job?' There's no doubt about the answer to that in your case. But the second question is, 'Why are you here?' It gets back to your asking about your role. If you don't persuade them to answer that question the way you want it answered, you probably can't get them to be cause leaders."

"I agree. They have to understand that I'm not there simply to communicate information, but to help them succeed in the restructuring. If an audience thinks that you can't help them or don't want to help them, that you're there simply for yourself, in effect you don't have an audience. But what's that have to do with my walking up to the dealership? If I describe it, they'll think I'm going off on a tangent about myself."

"It's not a tangent. It's central to your Leadership Talk, central to who you are. In a very real sense, why you're here in front of them is what you felt, what you experienced in your youth. This is a point most leaders miss. They think the most important things to communicate are their knowledge, skill, and position. Those are important, of course; but what's important too—most important of all—is the relationship. The answer to 'Why are you here?' develops and cements that relationship. Look at your case. You're asking them to help lead great change. Their choice to lead that change will involve many factors. One of those factors is, in no small measure, is the Leadership Talk you give them. In all likelihood, they won't begin to even think about making the choice to lead—at least when you're talking—unless they know why you're there giving the Talk."

"But in regard to the dealership experience, I'm talking about me, not them. They don't want to hear about me. They want to hear about *them*."

"Of course, they do. But by talking about where you yourself came from, you're really talking about them. You're talking about them in the most important way of all."

"The point is fuzzy."

"Here is the point. First, wouldn't you agree that they don't care about your problems, they care about *their* problems?"

"Of course."

"So, when your experience offers solutions to their problems, they'll not only be interested in that experience, but more, they'll also absorb that experience. It'll become their experience. With that in mind, let's take the fourth step in the motivational transfer process: Make your experience become a solution to their needs."

"Let's recap what you've been saying. Experience is a powerful way of learning. When my experience becomes a solution to their needs, there's a good chance that they will learn in a powerful way how to take new action."

"When it's a solution to their needs, your experience becomes a lens through which they view themselves and get new insights. Further, your experience in fact *becomes* them. Those insights prompt new actions. Now let's apply the principle to your situation. What's their big problem?"

"They have two big problems, the first is short term, and the second, long term. The short-term problem is that they might be anxious about what I'm going to say. They know we're making an announcement about a major restructuring. They might be wondering if they'll understand what I say, and if they understand it, agree with it. The long-term problem is, they might be anxious about the commitment they're going to make to the restructuring once they go back to their jobs."

"Why?"

"Because that commitment might cause them to go off in wrong directions. It might cause them to lose authority, lose control. It might tear up their lives both on and off the job. It might put their jobs and careers in jeopardy. Look, restructuring aside, these leaders are in a fight for their lives. It's not news that automotive manufacture is a dog-eat-dog industry worldwide. They have to work hard, they have to focus, and they have to keep the people they lead focused. Now we're doing this restructuring. They can't take time off from the fight to do restructuring. They have to get their results *and* restructure at the same time. They might think the ground of their careers is dropping out from under their feet."

"All the more reason that they need to know why you're there. Put yourself in their place. Wouldn't you want somebody who's passionately committed to the company giving you a Leadership Talk about the necessity for the restructuring? Wouldn't you want someone who's passionately committed to *you*—to your problems—giving you a Talk?"

"Of course. We have to hang together or hang separately. We have to be a band of brothers. It's only through a total commitment to the restructuring and to each other that we'll succeed in this. So, I see now how my experience can be a solution to their needs. Communicating that experience will make a huge difference in my Talk. In fact, it might make the defining difference. I see now what the Leadership Talk is: it's truly a motivational transfer."

"But you haven't gone far enough. You haven't gotten to the root need."

"I thought I had."

"In giving Leadership Talks, you should continually be asking, 'Have I identified the root need?' I think you can dig more."

"Let's dig."

"I've talked about how you can use a defining moment from your past to communicate experience. You used an experience that was closely linked to the company. But remember that a defining moment doesn't have to be job related. It can be any experience in your life, even childhood experiences. It doesn't have to be your experience. It can be the experience of someone you know or have heard of, and it doesn't necessarily have to be earthshaking. It can be one of life's little lessons. The key is that it should be an experience that provides a solution to your audience's needs. Moreover, a defining moment doesn't have to be communicated in words. It can be communicated through action. In the movie, when Mister Roberts threw the captain's palm tree into the sea, that was a defining moment of pure action. Now, let's get to the root."

"Keep digging."

"Put yourself in their place. You're in the audience, listening to you up there, speaking. The you in the audience is being challenged to take new action. Are your deepest needs being addressed?"

"If I were in their place, I'd be wondering if I was taking that action all alone, wondering if I'd get backing when things got tough."

"Right. If a leader motivates the troops to charge, but then watches the charge from a bunker, what does that say about the leader's relationship with the troops?"

"That the leader's more concerned about his or her skin than their welfare. That leader hasn't transferred belief. In fact, that leader has instigated anger."

"Doesn't your audience want to make sure you're with them, that you're their partner, that you'll share the risks with them, that you're jumping off a cliff together and making your wings on the way down?"

"That's it exactly. Their root need is to have me and the others speaking that day jump with them. Through information, logic, and the defining moment of experience, I transfer to them my belief about the risks that I'm taking with them. The difference between leaders might very well be the motivational transfer."

For a summary of how this Leadership Talk turned out, see Appendix B.

Lessons

Since the function of the Leadership Talk is not to order people to accomplish tasks but to motivate them to want to accomplish those tasks, motivation can't happen unless the leader's belief becomes the audience's belief. This is accomplished through the motivational transfer.

The motivational transfer is effected through the use of information, structure, and experience. The use of information and structure simply entails providing compelling information in a concise, organized, commonsense way that will persuade your audience to believe what you believe.

The use of experience entails the development and communication of the defining moment—a flash point of emotional experience that you communicate to your audience to help them make the choice to be your cause leaders for more results, faster, continually. The experience could be yours or that of someone you know or have heard of.

You develop the defining moment by recalling the physical facts of the experience that gave you the emotion. The most effective facts are actions. You communicate those facts to your audience by speaking, by taking action (throwing the palm tree overboard), or by engaging in a combination thereof. The defining moment doesn't necessarily have to be an "earthshaking" experience. It can be one of life's little lessons (see Appendix A).

The defining moment becomes ingrained in the audience's experience when it provides a solution to the audience's needs. The defining moment isn't a series of events. It's an actual moment of experience (see Appendix A). It must be a moment, because experience is best communicated through the expression of vivid moments.

The Motivational Transfer Process

Step One: Recognize

Know that you must not only bring passion to the talking situation but must also *have a passion to bring passion* to that situation. The executive's questions about his role stemmed from the fact that he hadn't taken this first step. Once he recognized the importance of his strong belief and the necessity for his transferring that belief to his audience, he began to understand that role.

Step Two: Identify

Identify the experience that gave you belief. It's not enough for us to feel it; we must know *why* we feel it. Otherwise, we won't be able to make the motivational transfer happen consistently. The best way to know *why* is to recall and examine our experiences that triggered it. The executive's strong belief in the necessity of the restructuring was rooted in powerful experiences. When he became fully conscious of those experiences, and conscious that they could help him realize the motivational transfer, he was well on his way to developing a Leadership Talk. It's not necessary to use experiences that happened on the job. Your whole life is a treasure house of useful experiences. During the past decade, while I've been teaching the motivational transfer to leaders from around the world, I've heard many experiences that effectively realized the transfer. Most of them derived from experiences outside the leaders' work environments, from when they were in high school, or in the military, or raising a family. It doesn't matter where the experience comes from, and doesn't necessarily have to be your own experience, though personal experiences may help communicate personal emotion. It simply has to work.

Step Three: Transform

Transform the experience into a defining moment. This means recalling the moment of the emotion and the physical facts that actually triggered the emotion.

Step Four: Transfer

Describe the defining moment to your audience. In their minds, it must play like a movie clip, a moment of physical action. The motivational transfer happens when the communicated experience furnishes a solution to the audience's need, so find out the lesson in the experience, and have that lesson be the solution to the problem embedded in the need. The lesson / solution makes the transfer happen. Without a lesson / solution, there'll be no transfer. Some experiences shouldn't be communicated. They fall into two categories: experiences that relate to private affairs, and experiences that relate to unintended communications. There's a difference between *personal* experiences and *private* experiences. Personal experiences should be communicated; private experiences kept to ourselves. To decide whether to communicate a private experience, ask yourself if it would embarrass you to describe it to others. If so, don't communicate it. Regarding unintended communications, the defining moment can be so powerful that you must be careful that you're not communicating an unintended message. If, for example, you tell people who are under threat of losing their jobs about how you were fired once and how it helped you reorder your life, your unintended communication, that *they* might be fired, could be more powerful than the lesson you draw from the experience. The executive surmised that his audience might be concerned about whether they themselves could understand and agree with the restructuring, and so be consistently committed to advocating it at work. His experience was a lesson / solution for those concerns. Let's be clear about the importance of that experience, as this is where most leaders stumble when trying to bring deep belief to the Leadership Talk. In fact, in terms of motivating people, it's where they stumble throughout their careers. That experience wasn't just something that happened years ago in another place; it was unfolding in his life right now. He felt and lived and dreamed it afresh. Standing before his audience, he was standing in that experience. He wasn't simply telling a story; there are crucial differences between a story and an experience—the defining moment being experience, not necessarily story. He :*was* that experience. To know this is to come to grips with a powerful leadership truth that's been manifested through-out recorded history, one that I've seen in my work with leaders of all stripes. If applied daily through Leadership Talks, this truth can make a great difference in the effectiveness of your leadership and your ca-reer. Also, no matter what the experience is, it usually holds a powerful lesson / solution for the audience.

Practice

Phase 1: Think of five defining moments in your past. Remember the embarrassment test: we're not talking about private defining moments; if you're in any way embarrassed about revealing the moment, keep it to yourself. A good way to come up with a defining moment is to think of times when you felt particularly strong emotions: anger, fear, joy. What events gave you those emotions? Identify the exact physical actions in a particular event that stimulated the emotions. I repeat: the defining moment is not a series of moments; it's a single moment, usually of physical action.

Phase 2: Use one of those defining moments in a conversation or speech. (You're not yet ready to put together a Leadership Talk. Later, I'll show you how to use defining moments in your Talks.) You might feel awkward at first employing the defining moment, but keep in mind that it's one of the most powerful leadership tools you can use. It's especially powerful when it provides solutions to the problems of your audience's needs.

Phase 3: Use one defining moment every day.

For a summary of how this Ladership Talk turned out, see Appendix B.

Action

Understanding the audience's needs and investing your Talk with strong belief are important, but not as important as action. Ultimately, it's not what you say in a Leadership Talk that counts, but what the audience does after you've had your say.

The head of a global business unit in a company that was trying to reinvigorate its growth worldwide told me that increasing business efficiencies was a key part of the growth strategy. She said, "We've benchmarked what it takes to be world class in those efficiencies. We've developed measurable objectives to shoot for. We've got great tactics. The trouble is, we're not getting there as fast as we have to."

"Speed is a great way to increase your results," I said. "But if they don't know where they're going, they'll resent going fast. And even if they know where they're going, they might think that in order to go faster, they simply have to go faster. But going faster to go faster usually causes people to slow down permanently."

"Yes. To become efficient, we first had to become *inefficient*. I understand that. We had to take a time-out, step back from what we were doing, and take a good hard look at things. In doing so, we developed good plans and processes. They're in place, we're working them, but still— "

"When you have good plans and processes but not good results, what do you focus on?"

"Execution," she said. "It can be a lot easier to develop strategies and tactics than to get people to execute them well."

"What are the key factors in execution?"

"The way I see it, there are three: understanding, skill, and action. They have to understand what to do, be skilled in what to do, and they have to damn well do it! The leaders in my unit are good in the first two, but falling down in the third."

"Then let's look at action within the framework of the Leadership Talk."

"Brent, I'm talking about action—you're talking about talking."

"Talking begets action. But for too many leaders, talking simply begets talking. If what you say doesn't trigger action, you really haven't given a Leadership Talk. Let's focus on getting your leaders to take actions that get the results you want. But before you even think of action, you must think of results. You must ask, 'Are we getting the right results?' There are right results and wrong results. It's been my experience that most leaders are getting the wrong results, or getting the right results in the wrong way. If you get people motivated to take extraordinary action for the *wrong* results, you'll wind up with few results and angry people. A good way to insure that you're aiming for the right results is to apply what I call the SAMMER test: Sizable, Achievable, Meaningful, Measurable, Ethical, Repeatable. Let me explain. Results should be sizable; they must be more, faster, continually. Results must be achievable—hard, but not impossible to achieve. Results must be meaningful; your cause leaders must be passionately committed to achieving them. Results must be measurable; you should quantify them to provide a standard of value, though this may not be possible in all cases. Results must be ethical; you achieve them with integrity and report on them honestly. Results must be repeatable; they should be springboards for even more results."

"I haven't thought about our results in terms of those criteria, but when I apply them, I'm sure we're aiming for the right results. We went to a great deal of trouble to focus on what it takes to be world class."

"Then let's take the next step, action. First, let's clear up the confusion about what action really is."

"Confusion? What's confusing? Action is action."

"There's right action, and there's wrong action. Right action leads to right results; wrong action leads to wrong results. Most leaders don't know the difference between right and wrong action. What's worse, they don't know that they don't know the difference."

"What's right action?"

"Right action is what helps get more results, faster, continually. Wrong action doesn't. It's as simple as that. When we talk about right action, we have to talk about it taking place in two different realms: one is the action that takes place when you're face to face with your audience, usually after you've given a call to action following your Leadership Talk. The other is the action that takes place when they're out of your sight. True motivation happens not just when you're talking with people, but when they're going about their business without you around. Right action shares the same attributes in both realms: Right action is physical. This may seem obvious, but most leaders don't challenge people to actually take physical action. I'll get into this later. Right action is purposeful. When people are taking action, they should be clearly conscious of the purpose of that action. Right action is honest. Don't trick people into taking action—you'll lose their trust. Right action is meaningful. The action people take should have meaning for them, and it will if it's providing a solution to their needs. So right action also helps solve their problems. Finally, when we talk about right action following your call to action at the end of a Leadership Talk, we should add two more attributes: that particular right action should take place immediately after you speak, and it should take place in your presence. Now let's apply the attributes of right action to the actions you need to take place."

"I need a lot of action in a lot of places."

"You're talking strategy now."

"Strategy's a broad brush."

"What's a Leadership Talk?

"It's a point, Brent."

"A point like in a pointillist painting?"

"You mean a lot of single points composing a complete picture?"

"Yes. And what's the picture we're talking about?"

"Results."

"And what gets the results?"

"The organizational dynamics of my business group. I see. Just as in pointillism, where each point is applied with regard to the whole, a lot of single-pointed Leadership Talks can compose broad, powerful organizational action. We need faster order-to-remittance cycles, so let's start there. It takes us far too long to process orders from customers, get products to customers, and then get payment. We've developed a streamlined order-to-remittance process to fix that problem. I've put a team in charge of the process. People are taking a lot of action. There are a lot of points being splashed on the canvas. But those points aren't coalescing into any picture of speed. Our people simply aren't making order-to-remittance happen fast enough—the execution affliction again."

"When you want a group of people to take action, first identify those people in the group whom you need to be your cause leaders for that action, and give a Leadership Talk or Talks to them."

"A Chinese philosopher / general said, 'The best victory comes without having to fight.'"

"That's the idea. You try to win those Talks with individuals before you interact with the group as a whole. Now let's go back to the right action that must flow from every Leadership Talk. Which particular leaders in your organization need to take action?"

"One in particular, a very important person in the department. He has unique expertise, people look up to him, and he's a natural leader. I strongly need for him to be a cause leader. The trouble is, for a lot of vague reasons, he's unhappy in the department. He doesn't get along well with several of his coworkers, and wants to transfer out. I'm reluctant to focus on him."

"Let's focus on him. When targeting potential cause leaders, don't shrink from those headstrong people who nevertheless would make great cause leaders. Be confident that the Leadership Talk will help you win them to your cause. Now, let's go back to basics; how do you get cause leaders?"

"By giving Leadership Talks."

"Let's see how you can motivate him—that is, have him motivate himself—to choose to be the cause leader for speed."

"Well, the first thing to think of when putting the Talk together is not what I want to say but what he needs to hear. O.K., he needs to get on board with my push for speed."

"Whose need is that, his or yours?"

"I see. That's *my* need. It might not be his need."

"What does *he* need?"

"He has a very strong need to be a leader with his peers. He likes to be looked up to as a leader. He craves that recognition."

"He'll only be motivated to be your cause leader when—"

"When he sees that I'm helping him solve the problem of his need. The problem is clear: How can he continue to be a strong leader and be recognized as such by his peers?"

"O.K., how?"

"You've stated this Leadership Talk rule many times: We should avoid solving people's problems for them. Instead, we support them in their taking the leadership to solve their own problems. But it must also be a solution to the business's needs. If it's a solution to the business's needs alone, he might not be totally committed to taking that action. If it's a solution to his needs alone, the business may suffer for it. But if it's a solution to both the business's needs *and* his needs, bingo!"

"Right. I call it critical confluence. But that's not all."

"He can't just tell me he's going to take action. I should know precisely what physical action he's going to take."

"For instance?"

"Since he wants to be recognized as a strong leader, I'll ask him what strong leadership action he'll take to help us get faster results. I'm asking *him* to define and declare his actions—his leadership actions. Clearly, he's going to be more committed to actions that he defines—provided that I can agree with him that they're the right actions."

"Yes. When you give a Leadership Talk and elicit from your audience what leadership actions they plan to take, you must agree with those actions before they take them. Your audience can't act any way they see fit. You can veto any action they propose. But I've rarely seen a leader have to veto audience-delineated actions. In most cases, they're pleasantly surprised by how effective those actions are."

"I should have been doing this for years. I *am* going to be doing this for years!"

"What's *your* role in all this?"

"First, to make sure that he takes the right actions. He doesn't have carte blanche to do whatever he wants."

"That's right. You have the veto."

"He and I have to agree on what he says he's going to do. But once we come to an agreement about those actions, I'll support him in taking them. I'll give him air cover, training, resources, the all-important recognition from his peers—whatever he needs, within reason, to be successful."

"And then?"

"Then we must agree on how we'll monitor and evaluate his actions."

"You've just described a five-step action process. Step one is to have him describe the leadership actions he'll take. Leaders go through their entire careers and fail to do what you just described. They tell people what action to take rather than first having the people themselves define that action. Your most powerful Leadership Talk is often not theirs to receive but theirs to give. Step two is to test the results. You can use your testing methods or apply the SAMMER test. Step three is to draw up a leadership contract. This can be written, or simply an oral agreement. It's not a legal thing; it's just a spelling out of the leadership actions you both agree he must take. This agreement is vital. He can't just take any actions that he sees fit. He and you have to agree on those actions. You can veto any of them. Moreover, make sure those actions are precisely described. Remember: motivation isn't what people think or feel, but what they do. Motivation is physical action. Have clear, physical actions come out of that contract. Step four is to detail how you'll support those actions. For example, you can remove barriers to his leadership and also give him and his own cause leaders special training or tools. Step five is to agree on how to monitor and evaluate those actions."

"So the process of defining action is as important as the action itself; because when you have the people themselves identifying and declaring and committing to action, there's a much better chance of their *wanting* to go from point A to point B."

"And thus of their moving from getting average results to getting more results, faster, continually."

"I see what you mean about action having to be physical, purposeful, honest, meaningful, and a solution to their needs. When my business team starts doing this, watch our smoke! But what do you mean by those other two attributes—that action must be immediate, and must take place in my presence?"

"Action takes place in space *and* time. When you come to agree on "what," you must also agree on "when." Granted, the action he commits himself to might take place at different times over months. But there's always action he must undertake immediately—right after you give your Leadership Talk."

"What's that action?"

"That's the action that he takes responding to your call to action. Remember the two realms, the action he takes following your call to action, and the action he takes after he leaves your presence. To understand how these two realms are separate and also related, let's go beyond the pointillism analogy. The sum of many Leadership Talks that challenge people to take specific, well-thought-out action can create powerful organizational action. That analogy was useful to help provide a preliminary idea of the relationship between the Leadership Talk and organizational action, but the reality of that relationship is richer and more dynamic than the simple representation of a painting. Leaders who can consistently understand that flowing, changing relationship, and use it to get results, will be far more successful in their jobs and careers than those who don't. The key to that understanding and use is a rule of the Leadership Talk: as soon as you finish talking, your audience must take some kind of action. They must know why they are taking that action. They must take it immediately. And you must see them take it. Only then will you begin to truly use the Leadership Talk to improve organizational action and results. To understand why, let's apply this rule to your cause leader."

"Okay, I'm going to give a Talk to tell him to take leadership in our order-to-remittance process."

"Oh, so you're ordering him to take leadership?"

"Of course. He doesn't have a choice. If I want him to take leadership action, he'd damn well better take it!"

"Many leaders would agree with you. That's why those leaders don't get more results, faster, continually. Let me ask you, is there a difference between doing a job and taking leadership of that job?"

"A big difference. When we do a job, we simply accomplish it. But when we take leadership of that job, we bring a higher order of motivation, initiative, action, and accomplishment to what we do."

"So challenging people to lead is better than simply challenging them to do?"

"Yes. But we all can't be leaders. Some of us have to be doers."

"I'm not talking about leadership position; I'm talking about leadership performance. After all, don't we best accomplish tasks when we take leadership? Position doesn't matter here. I could be talking about a floor sweeper. If that floor sweeper wanted to do the best floor sweeping, shouldn't he or she take leadership of floor sweeping?"

"Yes."

"Now let's go back to your ordering him to take leadership. If you order him, will he be motivated to lead?"

"Not necessarily, not when I'm ordering him."

"But isn't motivation a key aspect of leadership?"

"Of course."

"Can anybody motivate him to do anything?"

"No, he has to motivate himself."

"Since motivation and leadership are two sides of the same coin, isn't his leadership *his* choice—and no one else's? After all, isn't ordering people to take leadership nonsense? You might get average results doing that, but you won't get more results, faster, continually. Since motivation is not the leader's choice but the people's, getting such results happens in the realm of their free choice. If people could be ordered to get more results, faster, continually, organizations of order-leaders would never go out of business."

"All right. I can't order him to lead; he has to choose to lead. My Leadership Talk sets up the environment in which he makes that choice. But what if he doesn't make that choice?"

"If he doesn't make the choice to lead, your path is clear. You can either stop trying to get him to lead or you can keep giving Leadership Talks. Remember: they're *your* choices. There are people who'll never pick up your challenge to take leadership, no matter how well and how often you try. He might be one of those people. Then there are the rest, who won't take leadership simply because you've misread their needs. He might be one of them. In all likelihood, if you really nail his needs, he'll take leadership to solve the problem that they pose, because it's his leadership that can best solve his problem. Only you know when to make the choice to give up trying. But don't let failure make you quit on him. Even if you've given him many Leadership Talks, and he still won't take leadership, don't think you've failed. Failure is *your* choice. You only fail when you quit. So keep at it. Refocus. Re-analyze. Repeat. Thomas Edison said that his successes were built on countless failures."

"O.K., if he won't take the lead in getting faster order-to-remittance, my choice is clear, either stop trying or keep trying. If I stop, I'd better look for another potential cause leader. If I keep trying, I'll keep working the process, keep giving Leadership Talks. I understand. Now let's look at the other side. Let's say he does take leadership. What then?"

"That gets back to the rule of Leadership Talk that your audience must always take action right after you've given a call to action."

"Why?"

"Let's look at your situation. You've just talked to him about his taking leadership to get speed. In that interaction, you should have drawn a clear line. In every Leadership Talk, you draw a clear line. On one side of the line, he simply does; on the other side, he leads. He should be clearly conscious of where he stands regarding that line. *You* should be clearly conscious of where he stands. It's his choice to step over that line or not. Let's say that he has stepped over the line. He's committed to taking leadership. You've drawn up a leadership contract. It doesn't have to be complete at this point; it can be a partial contract. You might want to flesh out the full contract in the ensuing days. Still, this is a critical juncture, when many leaders let the audience off the hook, let them get away. The Talk is over, the meeting is finished, everybody goes his or her separate ways. If you're not careful, if you let him off the hook, he'll go back to his job and do pretty much what he's been doing all along. And that's usually not leadership. The trouble is, it's not his fault that he got off the hook, it's *your* fault; you haven't tested his commitment to take leadership by giving a call to action for immediate action."

"What can that action be?"

"Anything you want it to be. How he acts is less important than that he acts."

"Let me be clear about this. When I finish talking, he should start to do something? He should start to take some kind of action?"

"Immediate action always has to follow every Leadership Talk. You must see the action."

"And the form of that action is less important than its function?"

"Yes."

"And the function of that action?"

"To test and cement his commitment."

"O.K., let's say that I've given him my Leadership Talk. I've explained the importance of speed, and shown him how his leadership can help solve his problems. We've come to an agreement on the specific ways that he can take leadership to get speed."

"In other words, you've drawn up an informal leadership contract. Remember: the contract doesn't have to be completed right then and there. He might want to go out and talk with others about how speed might best be accomplished. Then he can get back to you later with a fleshed-out plan of action. But whether or not you complete the contract then and there, you must give a call to action.

"O.K. Just before I'm finished talking, I say, 'Do you agree with what I say? Do you agree that you should take the lead in this matter?' He might nod his head. He might say, "I agree, let's do this.' Is that the action you're talking about?"

"Yes."

"Through his body language, he communicates to me that he's committed to taking the lead."

"Yes. People's body language is often a more reliable—though not infallible—indicator of their feelings than their words are. But you might have more effective body language than just a nod."

"What about this? I finish my talk. I ask if he agrees. He nods his head. I then say, 'Why don't you get out your calendar and let's pick a date and time next week when we'll meet and you'll give me more details about the leadership you're taking?' He gets out his calendar."

"Physical action."

"He opens up the calendar."

"Physical action."

"He writes down a mutually agreed-upon date and time when we'll meet."

"While he's doing this, you're watching him. Is he anxious to get his calendar out, or reluctant? Might he say, 'I want to think about this?' and hesitate in writing down a date. All of these are tip-offs as to his commitment to leadership."

"And every Leadership Talk should end this way?"

"Every meeting, every Leadership Talk, should end with physical action of some kind."

"I might have him get out a piece of paper right there and write down three ways that I can support his leadership."

"Yes."

"I watch him take that action."

"Yes."

"And what if I read in the action I see him take that he's not committed as I want him to be? What if I read that he's reluctant or even recalcitrant?"

"Then get his reaction out into the open. Ask him about it. Have him describe that reaction. Ask him to be specific about its causes. Don't be angry—be interested. Get him talking. Get him giving you your Leadership Talk. Look, I'm not saying you'll be getting speed right then and there. My point is, without that immediate action taking place, the chances of speed happening later on when he's away from your presence will be considerably diminished. After all, if he leaves your sight, and you really don't know his true commitment to taking leadership, you've wasted your time and his. But if you test that commitment through immediate action, you'll have a pretty good idea of where he stands, and you can start working on problems while they're small and manageable, rather when they become big and overwhelming. From now on, throughout your career, try to have people take action immediately after every Leadership Talk. You'll infuse your interactions with clarity, simplicity, precision, and power. And those interactions multiplied many times—among all the others in your organization—help the organization as a whole achieve more results, faster, continually. And it all starts with the Leadership Talk and action stemming from that Talk."

"Pinning my organization's actions on actions taken at the conclusion of Leadership Talks seems pretty flimsy, Brent."

"It would be if that were all the action that you focus on. Remember: there's also the action that flows from the action process, which deals with the action he takes when he's not in your presence, over the weeks and months ahead. Have him describe the action, and then you agree with that action, contract for that action, support the action, monitor, and evaluate the action. With both those action-triggers working in tandem—immediate call to action and the action from the action process—speed will happen. All of this applies not only to your order-to-remittance process, but to all the results that you want to get."

For a summary of how this Leadership Talk turned out, see Appendix B.

Lessons

Strategies and tactics must be executed, and action drives execution.

Before challenging people to take right action, make sure you're trying to achieve right results. You can do that by applying the SAMMER test. Are the results you're aiming at Sizable, Achievable, Meaningful, Measurable, Ethical, Repeatable? Results should be sizable; they must be more, faster, continually results. Results must be achievable—hard but not impossible to achieve. Results must be meaningful; your cause leaders must be passionately committed to achieving them. Results must be measurable; you should quantify them to provide a standard of value, though this may not be possible in all cases. Results must be ethical; you achieve them with integrity and report on them honestly. Results must be repeatable; they should be springboards for even more results.

Action alone, however, isn't the objective of the Leadership Talk. There's only one objective of the Leadership Talk: to get cause leaders who take action to achieve more results, faster, on a continual basis.

There are two realms of right action: the action that takes place immediately after you give your audience the call to action, and the action that's prompted by the action process and takes place after your audience leaves your presence.

Right action is that action which achieves more results, faster, continually. Right action is physical, purposeful, honest, and meaningful. Right action also helps solve their problems. Moreover, when we talk about right action that immediately follows your call to action at the end of the Leadership Talk, we should add two more attributes: that right action should take place immediately after you speak, and directly in your presence.

The relationship between the Leadership Talk and organizational action is vital. Leadership Talks are points that, when aggregated and channeled, propel powerful organizational action along a broad front.

Before talking to the group as a whole, you might want to identify cause leaders within the group; give them Leadership Talks, and have them help you get more group cause leaders.

The five-step action process, the purpose of which is to have your cause leaders take right action after they leave your presence, follows.

Step One: Describe

Don't tell your audience what leadership actions to take to achieve more results, faster, continually. Instead, have them tell you what those actions should be. This helps cement audience motivation and leadership commitment.

Step Two: Test

Use a testing method, such as the SAMMER test, to determine whether you're aiming to achieve the right results.

Step Three: Contract

Come to a written or unwritten agreement, a leadership contract, on what those actions will be. The contract spells out the precise leadership actions that you and your audience agree will be taken. This agreement is necessary; you can't go forward without it. Your audience doesn't have carte blanche to lead any way they see fit. You can veto any action they propose.

Step Four: Support

Detail how you'll support those actions. Support can entail removing barriers to the audience's leadership, and providing them with the resources, such as training and tools.

Step Five: Monitor and Evaluate

Agree on how to monitor and evaluate that leadership. Action takes place in space *and* time. Focus not only on what's being done but also on when it should be done, and when and how you'll score or evaluate the action.

The purpose of the Leadership Talk isn't simply to have people take action, but to have them take leadership action. Taking leadership of a task achieves better results than merely doing that task.

- In terms of the Leadership Talk, leadership is not position; it's performance.
- The audience takes leadership action prompted not by your order but by their choice.
- Their action, prompted by your call to action, demonstrates the extent of their commitment to being your cause leaders.
- Their action, prompted by the action process, has one aim: to achieve more results, faster, continually.

If you failed to motivate them to take leadership action for your cause, you have either failed to clearly identify their need, or failed to show them how their leadership could help solve the problem of that need. Of course, there are audiences who'll refuse to take leadership for your cause no matter how well you do Leadership Talks. Approaching an audience that stubbornly refuses becomes a matter of where you spend your time, energy, and resources. You can select a new audience, or, if you're convinced that the audience is important enough to warrant the effort, you can persist in giving Leadership Talks to that audience.

Practice

Phase 1: Understand the connection between action and results by identifying the actions that you and others take to get results. One way to do this is to pick an enterprise you were involved with that achieved (or failed to achieve) targeted results. Apply the SAMMER test to see if you were aiming for the right results. Identify the physical actions that achieved results; identify the actions that failed to. Identify what actions should have been taken to get increases in results—actions as defined by the right actions of the Leadership Talk.

Phase 2: Draw an action flow chart showing the precise sequence of action that led to a particular outcome. Next, draw an action flow chart depicting what action should have been taken to achieve increased results. What lessons did you learn in comparing, contrasting, and correlating the two sets of actions? Apply those lessons to a future enterprise.

Phase 3: Select an enterprise by which you alone, or with a team, intend to get specific results. Apply the SAMMER test to the results. With the attributes of right action in mind, identify the actions needed to get those results. Now identify actions that will achieve *increases* in results. Understand the difference between the two sets of actions. Apply the lessons to future enterprises.

Section 2: Application

Bringing It All Together: The Landing

AT THE BEGINNING OF THIS BOOK, I likened the mental process of learning how to develop and deliver the Leadership Talk to free-fall parachuting. I said that your chute would open and you would land; that is, you'd come to the point where you'll put the concepts together and feel confident that you can begin giving Leadership Talks. Now you're at that point. You might at times have felt slightly perplexed and anxious until now, because you were learning things that didn't quite jell, but the free fall stops here. It's time to bring the concepts together, time to pull the ripcord. The chute will open, you'll have a "soft landing," you'll come to understand the Leadership Talk in its totality, and you'll find yourself in a new leadership place, surrounded by invigorating new opportunities. You'll be ready to get more results, faster, continually, by consistently using Leadership Talks—starting when you deliver your first Leadership Talk and continuing for the rest of your career.

What constitutes a soft landing is simply that you're ready to give Leadership Talks. Right now, I don't expect you to comprehend all the aspects of the Talk; you might still have questions; but know that they'll be answered during your experiences in regularly giving Leadership Talks. This confidence in being ready begins with learning a simple process to develop a Leadership Talk. The first step in the Leadership Talk process is to understand the key elements of motivation. Once you learn these, you can use them to create Leadership Talks.

The Motivational Elements

Since we can't motivate anybody to do anything, the motivators and the motivated are the same people. We communicate; *they* motivate—they motivate themselves. Only motivated people will choose to be our cause leaders, and they won't make that choice unless they know that their leadership offers solutions for the problems of their needs, not ours. In other words, a critical confluence of solutions / results, deeper and richer than simply win / win, must take place in order for a Leadership Talk to work. So, the Leadership Talk process involves your understanding the motivational elements, describing the needs of your audience, having them understand that the best way for them to solve the problems of those needs is to take leadership in bringing about solutions, linking that leadership and those solutions to more results, faster, continually, and supporting such leadership.

The Motivational Elements are signposts that help you compose the Leadership Talk. Every Leadership Talk must have at least three of these elements:

1. Need
2. Validation
3. Logical response
4. Defining moment
5. Support
6. Action

1. Need: People's needs are their reality Without your understanding their needs, without interacting with them in the framework of those needs, you can't give a Leadership Talk, because you fail to come to grips with their reality. Audience need involves the need / emotion / problem continuum. Understand each component of the continuum—the need, the emotion in the need, and the problem in the need / emotion. This is best accomplished by answering the Eight Needs Questions and choosing the answers that meet your challenge.

2. Validation: Just because you describe the need doesn't mean your audience will agree with that description. You must also validate, meaning come to an agreement with your audience as to what their needs truly are and how relevant their needs are in terms of getting more results, faster, continually.

In *Question 3, What action does the audience want to take?*, the line supervisor who'd been put in charge of eight opinionated employees had to come to an agreement with her audience regarding their needs. Without that agreement, she couldn't have motivated them to be her cause leaders. She said:

"Instead of going on about what the workers must change and how they should make those changes, and automatically believing that they're on board, I should have tackled head on the things that might be bothering them, like the fact that I'm perceived as an outsider, that they don't trust me yet, that they see management as their adversaries, that they fear having to change, and that they suspect this shakeup is a passing fad."

Coming to this agreement on what their needs are may take rigorous analysis. Sometimes your audience might not know precisely what they feel.

In *Question 7, What makes the audience angry?*, the operations leader said:

"First, they have to recognize that they're angry. That's not as easy as it sounds. I've found that angry people often don't want to face the fact that they're angry. Next, they have to tell me they're angry. We have to get their anger out on the table. If they keep it to themselves and don't convey it to me, then it'll just fester, and we're back to their being more committed to the festering anger than more results, faster, continually."

Once you've identified and agreed on their needs, you have to decide if those needs are relevant or irrelevant to achieving more results, faster, continually. In most cases, they're relevant. After all, since your audience's needs are their reality, you have to deal with that reality if you want to have them make the choice to be your cause leaders.

In *Question 1, What is changing for your audience?*, the plant manager

who wanted to get his boss out of his office first had to understand the
boss's needs and whether they were relevant to getting results. He said:

"The price he might think he has to pay is failure. Draw a circle
around all of those changes, and I see that my boss might be thinking
he's being set up to fail in trying to meet his boss's expectations. Higher
expectations, less resources—that's a prescription for failure, at least in
my boss's eyes."

However, there may be rare occasions when the needs of your audience
are irrelevant in terms of getting results. If you have to convince your
audience that those needs are irrelevant, you have a tough sell.

The sales and marketing leader of *Question 4, What does your audience
feel?,* affirmed this when she said:

"I had a boss who told me my feelings on the job were irrelevant and
to ignore them and just get the job done. I took his advice, but it got
me angry, because my feelings were me, and he was in essence saying I
was irrelevant."

That sell can be made, however, as long as you're working in the
realm of their needs, that is, when you have them see how they might
bring solutions to the problems of those needs. The operations leader
in *Question 7* told his logistics and administrative reports that they had
to move beyond their anger and "recognize that it's their choice to do
something about it. When they're solving the problems of their anger,
and I'm giving them the support to solve those problems, then they'll
more likely help lead my initiatives."

3. Logical response: Provide a logical response to the problem of their
needs. The logical response should include:

A. Analysis of the concrete factors that triggered the need

Be specific in the way that the supervisor in *Question 3* was specific when analyzing how her workers felt about her: "I'm perceived
as an outsider… they don't yet trust me yet… they see management
as their adversaries… they fear having to change… they suspect this
shakeup is a passing fad." In making such a precise analysis, she laid
the groundwork for a precise response. Furthermore, when you pre-

cisely analyze the roots of the need, you tend to precisely analyze its root problem—and are halfway to getting its solution.

B. The stakes

We can't convince people to be our cause leaders unless they and we agree on the stakes of the issue we confront. Stakes are what are gained or lost if action is or isn't taken. There are always stakes associated with every Leadership Talk. If your audience's view of the stakes differs from your view, you have a stakes' gap that must be closed. The telecommunications manager in *Question 8, What do they dream?* had a stakes gap. On one side of the gap, he felt that their good-old-days dream was severely handicapping their performance. On the other side, they felt that the good old days had to be restored. As long as that gap remained, he had no cause leaders.

In response to my asking, "What's their Major Problem?" he said: "Job security. They feel as if they're walking around with expiration dates printed on their foreheads."

"Does the good-old-days dream help them get job security?"

"Of course not. In fact, it prevents them from throwing themselves wholeheartedly into their present jobs—which might even screw up what little security they might have, if they have any, which they—we—probably don't. Just as I had to consciously realize what my dream was as a baseball player, and how it was affecting my life, so they must realize what their good-old-days dream is doing to their job performance. That's my job—to talk to them about it, to have them come to that realization, and then have them, not me, make the choice to change or not change. Those who choose to change, we can move forward together. Those who choose not to change, who still want to cling to the good-old-days dream, they and I have some work to do together."

C. A process to solve the problem of the need

First, define the problem in clear, precise language. Second, decide if it's the right problem, the one you want to solve; organizations stumble when providing diligent solutions to the wrong problems.

Test the problem by asking precisely how its solution helps get results. Use the SAMMER test to see if those are the right results to target. A solution linked to the wrong results is dealing with the wrong problem. Finally, put the process together. In most cases, work from upstream backward. Challenge your cause leaders to develop the processes themselves. People transform themselves by and through themselves. Their discoveries, their process developments, are more important to them than your discoveries and process developments. Help them help themselves. Help them take leadership for themselves and you.

4. Defining moment: I numbered this, but that doesn't mean it's in sequence. A defining moment can be put in any part of the Leadership Talk, wherever you need strong emphasis.

As the automotive executive said:

"Of course. We have to hang together or hang separately. We have to be a band of brothers. It's only through a total commitment, to the restructuring and to each other that we'll succeed in this. So I see now how my experience can be a solution to their needs. Communicating that experience will make a huge difference in my Talk. In fact, it could make the defining difference. I see now that the Leadership Talk is truly a Motivational Transfer. I see this not only as a difference in this Talk but really a difference in a career. The difference between leaders in their careers might very well be the Motivational Transfer."

Look for more defining moments in Appendix A.

5. Support: Describe how you'll support the leadership action your audience has committed to taking. As the business unit leader in the Action Section said:

"He and I have to agree on what he says he's going to do. But once we come to an agreement about those actions, I'll support him in taking them. I'll give him air cover, training, resources, the all-important recognition from his peers, whatever he needs, within reason, to be successful."

That support can take the form of removing obstacles to their leadership and providing special training and tools to help them lead more effectively.

6. Action: Know which realm of action you are dealing with: the long-term action associated with the action process or the short-term action associated with the call to action.

In terms of the long-term action, the leader in the Action Section said:

> "Since he wants to be recognized as a strong leader, I'll ask him what strong leadership action he'll take to help us get faster results. I'm asking him to define and declare his actions—his leadership actions. Clearly, he's going to be more committed to actions that he defines—if I can agree with him that they're the right actions."

"Yes. When you give a Leadership Talk and elicit from your audience what leadership actions they plan to take, you must agree with those actions before they take them. Your audience can't just act any way they see fit. You can veto any actions that they propose. But I have rarely seen a leader have to veto audience-delineated actions. In most cases, they're pleasantly surprised about how effective those actions are."

"I should have been doing this for years. I *am* going to be doing this for years!"

"What's your role in all this?"

"First, to make sure he takes the right actions. He doesn't have carte blanche to do whatever he wants."

"That's right. You have the veto."

"He and I have to agree on what he says he's going to do, but once we come to an agreement about those actions, I'll support him in taking them. I'll give him air cover, training, resources, the all-important recognition from his peers—whatever he needs, within reason, to be successful."

"And then?"

"Then we must come to agreement on how we'll monitor and evaluate his actions."

In terms of the short-term action triggered by the call to action, the leader said:

"What if I say this, then? I finish my talk. I ask if he agrees. He nods his head. Then I say, 'Why don't you get out your calendar and let's pick a date and time next week when we'll meet and you'll give me more details about the leadership you're taking?' He gets out his calendar."

"Physical action."

"He opens up the calendar."

"Physical action."

"He writes down a mutually agreed-upon date and time when we'll meet."

Every Leadership Talk must have at least three of the Motivational Elements: 1. Need; 2. Logical response; 3. Action.

There's no rigid sequence for using the Motivational Elements. Use any sequence that's most effective.

Recap: The Motivational Elements

Need

• Describe their need(s).

Validation

• Come to agreement with your audience as to the need, the emotion in the need, and the problem in the need / emotion.
• Is need relevant or irrelevant for getting results?
• If irrelevant, convince them why.
• If relevant, go to Logical Response.

Logical Response

• Analyze the factors that triggered the need.
• Define the stakes.
• Identify the problem in the need.
• Decide if it's the right problem to address. If so,
• Develop processes to solve that problem.

Defining Moment

• Nail down each important point with a defining moment.

Support

• Resources, administration, logistics, 360-degree communication, training, and upper-management commitment, etc.

Action

• Physical / Purposeful / Linked to Need / Immediate / Fed back.

The Leadership Talk Process

Now that you've learned the motivational elements that make up a Leadership Talk, it's time to learn the Leadership Talk process. Its objective is to help you consistently develop a Leadership Talk. You may use the process many times daily throughout the rest of your career. Here are the steps.

1. Decide to give a presentation or a Leadership Talk. There can be presentation aspects to your Leadership Talk, but you should decide if your communication is going to be fundamentally one or the other. Most of your communications should be through Leadership Talks, few through presentations. If you decide to give a presentation, however, go no further in this process. Use presentation methods, which are not in the purview of this book. If you decide to give a Leadership Talk, go to Step 2.

2. Identify their need(s) within the framework of the need / emotion / problem continuum. Before you start to think about what you'll say, think about what the audience needs to hear. They might not listen to what you say till you address what they need to hear. Identify what they need to hear by asking the Eight Needs Questions.

3. Select the appropriate answers and use them as your major talking points. You needn't use the answers to all eight questions; two or three—even one—might suffice. The rule is to use neither more nor fewer answers than you need. Use their needs as your major talking

points. In this way, you begin to promote the critical confluence and prepare the way for them to make the choice to be your cause leaders.

4. Flesh out the critical talking point(s) using the appropriate motivational elements. The talking points are the framework of your Talk; the motivational elements comprise the substance.

5. Deliver your Talk.

Recapping The Leadership Talk Process

Decide: Presentation or Leadership Talk? If presentation, don't go on. If Leadership Talk,

Identify: Need.

Select: One or more as your talking point(s).

Flesh out: The critical talking point(s) by using the motivational elements.

Deliver.

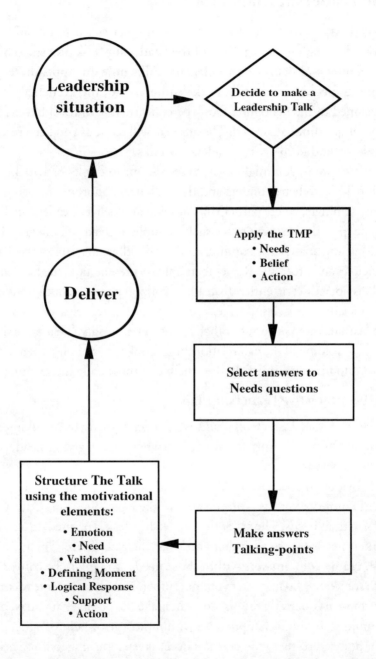

The Leadership Talk Process

THIS IS THE LANDING. THE FREE FALL SHOULD BE OVER. You should have a sound enough understanding of the Leadership Talk process to begin developing and delivering Leadership Talks now. In Appendix B you can find further clarification in the summaries of the Leadership Talks developed in the dialogues. Don't be concerned if you still haven't had all your questions answered. The answers will come as you keep reading this book and keep giving Leadership Talks.

At this point, you might want to see specific examples of actual Leadership Talks to better understand the Talk itself. Short of attending one of my seminars, where participants develop and deliver Leadership Talks on the spot, the best way to see such examples is to constantly give them yourself and analyze the communications of others in terms of the Talk's principles and processes. Remember: unlike a presentation, the Leadership Talk is not a discrete entity. Instead, it works as part of a continuous flow of interactions between people. I teach it as a discrete entity only so you can learn its mechanisms, but they're not its true reality. That takes shape in the unfolding of human relationships. Look for examples, then, in the most important venue of all, the crucible of those daily interactions.

The Interactive Leadership Talk

Most of your Leadership Talks won't occur when you're talking and your audience is simply listening, but when you're giving Leadership Talks conversationally. Here are tips.

1. Bridge to their needs. When asked questions, bridge to the audience's emotional needs—the answers to the eight questions. Always go back to their needs. The art of the Leadership Talk is painted on a canvas of their needs. Agree with them on what their needs are. Then,

2. Frame your answers within those needs. You might be conversing with someone who fears that your new program will cause her team to fail to achieve its quarterly results. You can make the points that you want to communicate about that program within the fear-of-failure frame. Link your points directly to their critical needs; keep returning to those needs, and your chances of having a successful exchange of ideas improve.

3. Have them give your leadership talks. Encourage the audience to talk about their needs as ways to get results. Those needs are problems that you and they provide solutions for; those solutions *are* results. Your audience can provide your most effective leader talks. Encourage them to be passionate about what *you* want to accomplish, and to communicate their ideas and their passion.

4. Quote them often. When they speak, remember what they say, so you can quote them later—to themselves and others. People listen intently when you're quoting them. People are well disposed to take action when it's triggered by their words. Make sure you get their permission to quote them; then quote them accurately and in a way that shows them in a good light. Honor them their words, and you increase the likelihood that they'll become your cause leaders.

5. Use their needs as tools for results. Their needs are their world. You have no other means of motivating them but in the opportunities that world offers. Use their needs as lenses to view the challenge before you. For example, "You're angry that you're not being listened to by upper management. What are the precise reasons they aren't listening?" Use their needs as signposts that point to new processes. For example, "What are ways that we can get better results so they have to listen?"

6. Don't give updates or briefings; give Leadership Talks. See each leadership challenge you face as an opportunity to motivate people to take action for results. Don't provide information alone. Look for the motivational elements in the information and use them to give Leadership Talks.

7. Don't be a messenger. If your audience thinks you're merely relaying information from a higher authority, they'll look upon you as a messenger. When the people you lead see you as a messenger, they may see themselves as victims. When they do, your leadership is blighted; people who believe they're victims can't get more results, faster, continually. The remedy is leadership. Continually motivate them to lead, and motivate them to motivate others to lead. Even though upper-management directives may give little room to maneuver, there are still many benefits that you, as a leader, can bring to them.

8. Know that all roads lead to leadership. At heart, every issue is a leadership issue. The defining concept of good leadership: *Leaders lead well only when the people they lead are leading well.* If you turn discussions back to leadership, and have strategies, processes, resources, and motivational skills tied to that defining idea, in most cases, you'll get to the core of the discussion. Challenge people by challenging them to lead others.

9. Be aware of stakes gaps. Whenever there's a heated discussion, a clarification of stakes often contributes to a resolution. Stakes drive urgency and commitment.

10. Encourage people to talk about their successes. Few people avoid talking about how they succeeded in any endeavor. You're not encouraging them to brag—most people are uncomfortable bragging about their accomplishments. Instead, encourage them to teach the processes and lessons of precisely how they succeeded. In an interactive exchange, you might say, "I know you disagree with my wanting to go to the mountain, but you got results by leading your team to another mountain. Mine is very similar to that one. How did you get your team to that mountain? What did you learn that would help us get to this mountain?" Don't just encourage people to talk about what they did that was great—encourage them to talk about how they did it.

11. Communicate the polarity of ideas. Every idea has a rational pole and a passionate pole. Communicate both. Talk to people's reason but also to their heartfelt convictions.

Doing It

The way we learn is often more important than what we learn. The "what" may be an abstraction, but the "way" is usually involves an experience. So it is with the Leadership Talk. Its meaning is its doing. Some leaders have jumped not wisely but too well into giving Talks, gotten discouraged, and quit. The reasons are many: the "fad-diet" phenomenon, lack of support, lack of good feedback, and the attack of the organizational status quo. The cultures of every organization I've encountered revolve around a status quo of presentations and order-leadership. Starting to give Leadership Talks in your organization will be like bringing a single lamp into a cultural hurricane. To keep your lamp lit, and to light the lamps of others, you must have the leadership equivalent of a hurricane lamp, which is a sound process for continually developing and delivering Leadership Talks. The following is a process that's working for many leaders who are keeping their lamps alight in the teeth of powerful cultural blows.

Phase 1: Give one Leadership Talk a day for thirty-five days. Don't give more than one talk a day, and don't skip a day. Consistency is the thing. Keep a diary reporting on whom you talked to, the information you developed in applying the Leadership Talk Process, and the results of the Talk. Pay special attention to short- and long-term actions taken by your audience, and the results obtained by that action. What worked? What didn't? How can you improve each Talk?

Phase 2: Give two Talks a day for thirty-five days. Don't give more than two a day or fewer than two. Keep the consistent effort. Follow through on the diary you used in Phase 1. Toward the end of this phase, you should be seeing significant increases in your ability to motivate people to become your cause leaders—and achieving more results, faster, on a relatively consistent basis.

Phase 3: Give many Leadership Talks per day, day in and day out, for the rest of your career. Since you do nothing more important as a leader than get results, aim to achieve more results, faster, continually, through your Talks. Enhance your mastery of the Leadership Talk through constant learning, applying, and teaching.

Mastery of the Leadership Talk isn't about being eloquent but about being yourself. You yourself are eloquence enough and eloquence itself. However, it usually takes years to master the art of being who we truly are when faced with the challenges of leading people. You've probably known many leaders who are excellent talkers as themselves but lousy speakers as leaders. I've heard of a superb Leadership Talk given by a crew chief to a crew member while they were being themselves, sitting on the back of a pickup truck, sipping beers at a company picnic. A dedication to learning, applying, and teaching is your road map to such mastery.

Learning: The Leadership Talk is simple to learn, but it takes many years to master, and even when you master it, you can still improve. Throughout the years, reread this book. Dip into it whenever the need arises. You can never learn too much about the Leadership Talk, which means you can never learn too much about human motivation. To this end, keep the diary active. Record whom you spoke with, the circumstances, what worked and what didn't with each aspect of the Three-Trigger Motivational Process, and why.

Applying: As you give Leadership Talks daily, your leadership abilities will become increasingly strong and supple. Your daily leadership efforts will become a kind of active meditation. You'll start talking and taking action from stimuli welling up from profound reservoirs of energy and understanding. Just as great athletic efforts happen on a subconscious level that can only be drawn upon after long practice, your best Leadership Talks will happen when you interact with people after the methods have been ingrained, not just into your thinking processes, but into your character and the way you live.

Take tennis, for example, though any sport will do. To play well, you must repeatedly practice the right methods of striking the ball, so your actions come naturally and unthinkingly in a real match. Getting to the point where you can give Leadership Talks naturally in the volleying of daily interactions takes a lot of practice and application. But you'll find that such efforts pay big dividends when your communications come to suit the circumstances and the needs of the people involved. Achieving more results, faster, continually, will unfold organically in your daily leadership activities. You'll talk less and listen more (as you've seen, the Leadership Talk is a listening process as well as a talking process). You'll understand that your most powerful Leadership Talks often happen when you ask questions of your audience and let their answers be your Talks. That's called giving "listening Leadership-talks." Furthermore, you won't have to sweat for solutions—you'll find that your cause leaders will often come up with the best solutions.

Clearly, you won't avoid difficulties. They come with leadership. If there were no difficulties, there'd be no need for leadership. But you'll come to see difficulties not as obstacles but solutions. Eventually, people will come to see you and relate to you in wonderful new ways; and when they do, they'll take new action for you and for themselves.

Teaching: The Leadership Talk becomes an even more powerful results-achieving, career-building tool when you use it not for yourself alone but when you teach it to others. The best leaders are good teachers. The ultimate measure of your leadership isn't simply your leadership but the leadership of your cause leaders. In teaching the Leadership Talk to others, you improve them and yourself as well.

Just as you must have a passion to achieve more results, faster, continually, so you must have a passion to teach the Talk. Teach the same sequence of steps that you find in this book; it offers the best method to have people come to understand and apply the concepts. You might start off with a general discussion of the difference between the presentation and the Leadership Talk, and then move into the Three Trigger Motivational Process. Make sure that those you teach understand each trigger before moving to the next. You could even use the analogy of free fall. Your "pupils," who may be not only the leaders who report to you, but your colleagues and even your bosses, shouldn't expect to understand the Talk immediately. There must be some free fall, some exposure to the basic concepts, before the chute of understanding opens, before you can bring it all together, and they can accomplish their own landing and start giving full-fledged Leadership Talks themselves.

Teach by asking questions and letting their answers be the instruction. Teach by having people practice a lot. Teach by showing how the Leadership Talk can help them in their jobs and careers. Finally, have your cause leaders teach the Leadership Talk to their cause leaders, so a cascading of Talks can saturate your organization. Keep asking yourself:

"How can I learn more today?"

"How can I better apply the Talk today?"

"How can I teach and coach today?"

The Leadership Talk is ultimately not a technique or even a process, but a high calling that summons you to share in the aspirations of others. To that end, believe in the power of people to transform their world and yours.

Appendix A

Model defining moments

THE DEFINING MOMENT IS THE DRIVE SHAFT OF THE LEADERSHIP TALK. It encompasses what getting more results, faster, continually is all about—establishing powerful human relationships. Remember the leadership principle I talked about earlier: *When people need to accomplish great things, a leader first has to gather them together and speak from the heart.* Defining moments further this principle in concrete, process-centered ways to help you repeatedly create the motivational transfer.

Yet, the vast majority of leaders I've initially encountered have, until then, been failing to use defining moments in name or in concept. There are several reasons for this failure: they're reluctant to talk about themselves; they believe that their audience will think they're bragging or trying to manipulate emotions; they want to keep their private lives private. Dealing with the defining moment is like handling nitroglycerin: if you mishandle it, if you communicate the wrong things, it'll blow up in your face; your audience will be turned off. But just as stabilizers can make the chemical useful in dynamite and rocket propellant, so the explosive defining moment, when stabilized, will serve you well throughout your career. The stabilizer can be summed up in one word: solutions. When it provides solutions to the needs of your audience, its explosive effects will work for you, not against you.

Furthermore, you can have a great defining moment and use it as a solution to your audience's needs, but if that audience thinks you're using it as a technique, you'll fail to gain them as cause leaders. In organizations where the Leadership Talk is widely used, audiences are sometimes on the lookout for people ineptly applying the defining moment as a raw technique. If the audience chirps, "You're pulling a defining moment on us!" you haven't created an environment conducive to motivation. My advice is, cultivate the art of hiding the defining moment. It shines brightest out of sight. Use it so people aren't overtly aware of it. Make it a seamless part of your communication. One way is to frame it. You tell your audience that you'll talk about an experience, and why—because it will provide a solution for you're their needs. You communicate the experience. Then say why you communicated it, explicitly stating the problem and the solution gained from the experience. There are many more artful ways to employ defining moments. You further the art through diligent trial and error. Since great results happen through relationships predicated not on your ordering people about but having them become your ardent cause leaders, it behooves you to do all you can to be the kind of leader who consistently establishes those relationships. When the defining moment expresses the better part of you, it will help your audience believe in, and take action from, the better parts of themselves.

The following are a few defining moments that I've encountered. Most entail powerful experiences, but good defining moments derive not just from the rare experiences but also from the daily, mundane encounters. Just living our day-to-day lives, we're saturated with defining moments. You can look at them as life's little lessons. Here's what happened to me recently on my way to giving a seminar.

1. I had breakfast in a diner where the waitress went to great pains to wipe off the counter and place the utensils. I've seen countless waitresses do this over decades, but this woman, in her forties with sparkling gray eyes, made that formerly mundane action seem special, as if I were the most important person in the world to her at that moment. Others came in and sat at the counter, and she did her work with the same painstaking attention.

2. In the cab I took to the company's headquarters, the driver, a young man from Armenia, said he was between jobs. "I went broke

owning a clothing store. I'm driving a cab to save money to start a new business. America is not just the land of opportunity, it's the land of opportuni*ties.* Maybe it's the only place in the world where you can keep reinventing yourself."

3. At reception, I asked the guard where I was supposed to sign in. He was sitting behind the desk with his feet up. "It's too early. The receptionist hasn't come to work yet. She'll be here in a few minutes."

"Can't you tell me how to go about signing in?"

"Nope," he said. "I don't have to do anything but sit here and breathe fresh air."

You can draw your own lessons from my three defining moments, but the ultimate lesson is that defining moments appear in our lives incessantly. You can use these defining moments as models to help you develop your own moments or those of people you know or hear about. Don't look at them as simply interesting anecdotes. Defining moments aren't meant to be stories. They're flash points of experience that can be transferred to other people through the motivational transfer process, so your experience becomes their experience; in that shared experience, cause leaders are born.

"I was a sprinting champion in high school, and really stuck up about my accomplishments. Then I broke my leg in a skiing accident. After it healed, I was playing softball. I hit a line-drive single to right field—and was thrown out at first base by the outfielder! What a pitiful sight: I was trying to run all out, but chugged slowly up that first base line. I saw then that the person I thought I was—a champion sprinter—no longer existed. I realized I had to become somebody else. I turned myself from an individual competitor into a team competitor. I went from stardom to "team-dom." Getting injured was the best thing that ever happened to my career."

— *Business school professor*

"I grew up poor. I was constantly angry with my mother for feeding us bologna sandwiches. Then one day I saw a half-eaten can of dog food under her bed. She was eating dog food to save money so we could have bologna. I never complained to my mother after that. And I think I stopped complaining in life, period!"

— *Boxing promoter*

"My senior year in high school, a teacher asked the class, "Who's going on to college next year?" I saw my friends raise their hands, so I raised mine, too. Trouble was, I had a terrible secret: I couldn't read well. I'd always had trouble reading and had taken mostly shop courses. That was the worst feeling I ever had. Raising my hand, I knew I couldn't make it in college. I was right. I flunked out. Had to join the army, where I shoveled coal in Germany for four years. But that's where I taught myself to read. I went on to graduate from Harvard. I've made it this far because my career hasn't been a series of jobs. It's been a vow that I would do my best in my life never to have someone feel what I felt when I raised my hand all those years ago."

— *Editor-in-chief of a major publishing company*

"As a child, I was watching a vaudeville show. When the performance was over, we all got up to give the troupe a standing ovation. But I didn't face the stage. I turned around and faced the audience. I remember thinking, *This is what I want my life to be. I want to stand and face an applauding audience!*"

— *Jackie Gleason, entertainer*

"I was brought up on a farm. One very hot day I was distributing and packing down the hay, which a slacker was constantly dumping on me. By afternoon, I was completely exhausted. That afternoon, I left the farm never to return. I haven't done a day's worth of hard work since."

— *Clarence Darrow, lawyer*

"I was an officer in the air force during World War II. Early in the war, a general came to inspect my squadron. He wrote 'Splendid!' on the report. That one word turned my life around. Until then, I had worked at IBM, and whenever I was complimented, I thought it was because I was Tom Watson's son. That 'Splendid!' was the first compliment I got for work that I alone was responsible for."

— *Thomas Watson, Jr., IBM*

"Sixty years ago, in Budapest, my father took me to an elegant restaurant. There, we sat beside a beautiful woman. She was a stranger. I never forgot that powerful experience of being in a fine restaurant beside a beautiful woman. After communism fell, I *had* to open my own elegant restaurant in Budapest."

— *Hungarian restaurateur*

"In Vietnam, my squad was ambushed by Vietcong. I was the only one who survived. I was hiding in brush when the Vietcong soldiers filed past me to leave the area. The last soldier turned and looked at me. He spotted me. All he had to do was pull the trigger and I was a dead man. But he did something incredible: he turned and kept walking. He could have killed me, but he gave me my life. Since then, I have tried every day to give something to people. My life has been one of service. That's why I got where I am."

— *CEO of a manufacturing company*

"My cancer-ridden father was experiencing a long, slow death, but because of hospice care he was relatively free of pain, so we had opportunities to have long conversations. It was at a time in my life when I felt particularly hopeless about my career. I told him I had run out of opportunities in business. He smiled, this man who once weighed 200 pounds and was now a ninety-pound skeleton; this man who was two weeks away from death smiled and said, 'Don't believe that for a minute. We all have opportunities. Look at me, even *I* have opportunities right here and now.' I never forgot that. It was the most powerful business lesson I ever had. I've known since that if on his deathbed my father could speak of his opportunities, then we never run out of them. They are always there, no matter what circumstances we are in."

— *Author and businessman*

"'Take your jacket off and be yourself!'"

— *Talk-show host Larry King*
(defining-moment advice given to him by Jackie Gleason)

"We're losing by one. The Soviets have the ball. The clock's running out. I hide behind the center, bait a guy into throwing a pass, knock it loose, and grab it. A Russian goes under me as I'm going up for the lay-up. I'm KO'd for a second. The coaches run to me. John Bach, one of the assistants, says, 'We gotta get somebody to shoot the fouls.' But Coach Hank Iba says, 'If Doug can walk, he'll shoot.' That electrified me. The coach believed in me. I can't even remember feeling any pressure. Three dribbles, spin the ball, toss it in, same as in my backyard. I hit 'em both and got the lead. I didn't know what I was made of until then."

— Doug Collins, member of the '72 U.S. Olympic team that ultimately lost the gold medal to the Soviet Union on a disputed call

Appendix B

Outcomes

These are summaries of the Leadership Talks that resulted from the dialogues in the Concepts section. Summaries, not verbatim reports, will suffice; it's not the saying that's the most important thing in a Leadership Talk but *their doing after the saying*.

Furthermore, that "doing" might happen without your having to say much. Often, the best Leadership Talk isn't what comes out of your mouth, but what comes out of the mouths of your audience. This can happen through "listening Leadership-talks"—you listen as your audience gives you your Talk.

So, the summaries will entail not only what the leader said but also what the audience said and ultimately did.

Needs

Question 1: What's changing for the audience?

Issue: Getting his boss out of his office

The Talk: The analytical mechanisms of the Leadership Talk can show you not only what to say and whom to say it to, but what *not* to say and whom *not* to say it to. Doing a needs analysis helped him understand that to have his boss choose to get out of his office and stay out—the problem of the need that surfaced in the answer to the question *What is changing for your audience?*—would have to be identified and solved. After all, his boss was running scared, chased by the new CEO's mandate of "more with less," and was trying to do practically everybody's cost-cutting job himself. The manufacturing leader, by answering the question, realized that his boss in his face was the symptom, not the problem, and that the solution involved a more comprehensive approach to reducing cost structures than simply cutting costs. It involved increasing operations efficiencies. He decided that the best Leadership Talk he could give boss to get him out would be not to talk to him about it at all. The increased operations efficiencies would do all the talking. He knew that to get those increases, he would have to deliver Talks to other people instead—cause leaders in his plants whom he needed to help make such efficiencies happen.

Under his light supervision, his cause leaders conceived of and directed a campaign to bring their operating efficiencies up to world class levels. They benchmarked the efficiency indexes of world class manufacturers, identified gaps between their operations and those manufacturers, set about closing the gaps—and started getting the resulting efficiencies. "I never did tell my boss to get out of my office. After a while, he did it all by himself. How sweet it is getting rid of the disease—and the symptom too!"

Question 2: Whom would they rather have speaking to them besides you?

Issue: Introducing a new quality initiative that the CEO wants disseminated

The Talk: We blur the distinction between messenger and leader at the leader's expense. Deciding not to give a presentation, which would have been a messenger's communication, but a Leadership Talk instead, he began the process of transforming his relationship with the audience. The first part of his Talk was devoted to his getting their feelings they would rather hear from the CEO than from him out in the open. He listed a David Letterman-like "top five" individuals whom they absolutely did not want to hear from—and made himself number one. Their laughter validated their feelings. Then he began focusing on their needs. Knowing that the aim of the Leadership Talk is to get cause leaders for more results, faster, continually, and knowing that people would be his cause leaders only if they saw that he wasn't just a walking brochure but embodied a solution for their own problems, he focused on formulating solutions to the problems of those needs. He told them how he'd help them accomplish the quality initiative in the right way, so they wouldn't waste time in rework. He told them he could help them streamline their training in the initiative and help them integrate the initiative into their present jobs so they would get more results. He showed them that *their* leadership would make this initiative succeed, and that he'd support their leadership by giving them the right resources at the right time. That change in relationship, from his being perceived as a messenger to being their partner for results, was the difference between the lightning bug and the lightning.

Question #3: What action does the audience want to take?

Issue: Getting the hidebound workers to change the way they did their jobs in order to achieve increased operations efficiencies

The Talk: If we don't define the reality we face for the people we lead, they'll define it for us—and we might not like the reality they define. This is often revealed in answers to this question. The supervisor hadn't defined reality for her opinionated charges, so they continued taking action to sustain their own reality. She began to change their reality and hers only when she began to give Leadership Talks. She said, "Instead of telling the workers that they must change, and how they should change, and automatically believing they would change, I tackled head-on those things that bothered them. Things like the fact that I'm perceived as an outsider, that they don't trust me yet, that they see management as their adversaries, that they suspect this shakeup is a passing fad—or worse, that it'll jeopardize their jobs. I had them see that adhering to the status quo way of doing things would mean that the plant might fall farther behind in its competition with the newer plants to be the low-cost producer. I had them see that the solutions to those problems lay not just with me or the company but with them and their taking leadership to get the solutions. That wasn't just one Talk. I'm having many Talks with them.

At first, a couple of them resisted. They said that I was the leader, not them; that 'it all pays the same,' and that until there was leadership in their job descriptions, they wouldn't take any leadership. But I kept giving Leadership Talks, kept clarifying their needs (listening as much as talking), kept showing them how badly their leadership was needed. I kept at it until all of them except one (I haven't yet decided what to do with him) agreed that our working together—really working together, not head-faking, not saying one thing and doing another—was in their best interests. I asked them to propose some leadership actions to do things more effectively. I told them they couldn't just take any action they wanted; that we both had to agree on the actions they proposed. That wasn't a problem. They came up with great actions. We agreed on phase lines and on ways to evaluate those actions. Now we're in the process of carrying them out. As for the one guy who won't do this, who won't take leadership, I'm hoping that he'll soon come along, meaning that the others will persuade him, or I'll have to take drastic action. I just can't let him be—he's constantly trying to pull the others back into his orbit, so something has to be done about him. I'm still working on that. I'm still working the whole thing out. It's not clear and simple. Sometimes it's messy, sometimes I'm going backwards, but I've got a process that I'm working, the Leadership Talk. And it's working. There's nothing magic about it. It takes a lot of hard work, but at least I'm headed in the right direction."

The supervisor's efforts point out the speed the Leadership Talk can engender. Some leaders might argue that going through the trouble of understanding others' needs slowed things down and wasted her time and theirs. But in fact, the supervisor's initial way of turning the situation around, which was essentially an order-leader's way, was the *slow* way of doing things. She was doing a lot of ordering but not getting results. The fast way was to first slow down and take the time to do Leadership Talks. Leaders who don't get this won't get more results, faster, continually.

Question 4: What does the audience feel?

Issue: Establishing trust

The Talk: A key reason that organizations and individuals fail is "fatal vision." Executives think that managers can change and managers think that executives will never change. The executive was about to say and do the wrong things before the Leadership Talk came to help out. After all, her leadership should be measured on what the leadership of all leaders should be measured on—not just on how well she leads but on how well the people she leads can lead. And she couldn't lead them to lead well as long as she felt one way about those nose-diving numbers and they felt another. She felt that the numbers should motivate them to do better; they felt the numbers demonstrated that the previous executive team had set them up to fail. Understanding that the gap between her feelings and theirs had to be closed, she decided to have a series of meetings with individuals before the big meeting with the group. Those individual Talks consisted of her allowing them to get their distrust of her and the company out in the open, to identify its root causes, and then elicit specific ways that they believed trust could be regained individually and as a group. When she got them all together, brought out the numbers, and gave a Talk (using that invaluable Leadership Talk tool, the question mark, to get them talking), their desire to put the past behind them and get on with turning the situation around replaced their feelings of betrayal. The numbers hadn't changed. She had learned not to hamper people by leading them, and had set up an environment in which they made the choice to change their attitudes about the numbers. Her work was only beginning, but she'd made the right start.

Question 5: What does the audience fear?

Issue: The crusade

The Talk: Most leaders are confused followers, and the smoke of confusion often has a high fear content. Let's use fear to deal with fear: we can use fear to promote clarity and courage; when ordinary people solve the problems of their fears, they can be blessed with new opportunities to do extraordinary things. The financial leader came to understand that the people felt that their accomplishing the extraordinary would sabotage their job security. The status quo—even an irritating status quo—is a tough addiction to kick. "If fear is their problem," he said, "it's a problem that needs a solution, and the best solution will invariably come from them. *Their* good solution is far better than my great solution."

He asked them outright if they believed the crusade would jeopardize their jobs. He had them identify solutions and the action they would take to execute and evaluate the solutions. He had *them* play a major role in developing the crusade. "If they aren't motivated to join my crusade," he said, "they'll be motivated to join *their* crusade."

Question #6: What is the audience's Major Problem?

Issue: Lack of self-confidence

The Talk: A common leadership failing entails leaders being absorbed in what they need from their people and oblivious to what their people need from them. This difference in focus can lead to big differences in results.

When I first met with the new CEO, he was thinking a lot about himself, his difficulties in having to replace the star, how he wanted to give a presentation on the state of the business, and the actions he planned to have his lieutenants take to improve results.

I suggested he apply the Leadership Talk rule of first thinking of what his audience needed to hear before thinking of what he needed to say. He discovered that their needs were connected to their Major Problem, rooted in the fact that the beloved, departed CEO had been a command-and-control tyrant. Even his subordinates' insignificant decisions had to be referred to him. Believing that his leaders were interchangeable, he trusted no one to take leadership but himself. Leadership should be measured not only by what you do, but also by what you leave behind; his departure left behind leaders whose focus wasn't on more results, faster, continually, but on the self-limiting mantra *How can I not screw up?*

The CEO's Leadership Talk was far different from the presentation he'd planned; he not only challenged them to get more results, but also asked them to delineate comprehensive, systematic ways to help them take leadership to get those results. It might seem a small difference, but it made a big difference in his Talk and in the results they subsequently achieved. When the people's needs and the solutions to them become the leader's passion, the people's passion becomes the leader. He became the change he wanted them to accomplish. He made a passion of helping them develop as leaders, and perfected the effects of that passion in many ways, small and large. He made his leadership a transparent model by holding frequent "town hall" meetings and routinely meeting informally with all the company's leaders. He insisted that they hold their organizational equivalents of such meetings. He made himself and his leaders accountable for results—no excuses. He got them educated in the right and wrong ways to lead, and had them make the development of leaders at all levels a high priority. He developed a culture of small-unit leadership excellence.

His delving into their needs didn't oblige him to pander to those needs. His company had to achieve increases in results—a fact that couldn't be compromised. He didn't lower the results-expectations. Given their shaky convictions, they might have wanted to. In this case, seeing wasn't believing; believing was seeing. He aimed for the same results, but got there in much better and faster ways.

Question #7: What makes the audience angry.

Issue: Having angry people make the choice to be one's cause leaders for more results, faster, continually

The Talk: Anger is the door prize of leadership. It's braided into most leadership challenges, because they usually require people to do what they don't want to do. But the function of the Leadership Talk isn't to get people to do what they want. If you want to motivate people to do what they already want to do, you wouldn't need to give them Leadership Talks. The Talk is about having people do what they often don't want to do, and be the cause leaders for doing it.

The operations leader was challenging the logistics-and-accounting employees to engage in what they didn't want to do, be partners with "the enemy," the people in other functions. The idea that they were second-class citizens might have come from real or imagined origins, but what was indisputably real was their anger, which the leader couldn't ignore. After all, that anger was causing them to champion the notion that the more-results-faster initiative was a waste of time. Yet, he had the double difficulty of being separated from them by a reporting layer of leadership. The reports of their anger and spreading of dirt were coming from roundabout sources, not from where it should, the leaders who reported directly to him. If he confronted the people directly, those leaders would think he'd gotten the information by going behind their backs. So, he decided to give Leadership Talks to enlist those very leaders as cause leaders who in turn would get the employees as cause leaders. This cascading of cause leaders is a force multiplier. The Talk is powerful in itself; but it's even more powerful when you achieve the cascading—cause leaders giving Talks to get more cause leaders. He had them engage in comprehensive needs analyses that identified the employees' anger. He had them draw up a leadership contract with the employees, challenging them to take leadership to bring solutions to the problems of their anger. He had the cascading network of cause leaders come together to develop measurable goals, monitoring and evaluation systems, timelines, and milestones—and then had them take meticulous actions to accomplish them.

Question # 8: What does the audience dream?

Issue: A toxic dream

The Talk: Touching the naked ends of the leader's vision and the people's dream hot-wires motivation, but if dream short-circuits vision, organizational fuses blow. The manager was faced with a common problem that crops up during workforce reductions: angry and dispirited people. In such a case, leaders can look to the anger or the low spirits for solutions, but often the most powerful solution lies in what the people dream.

Before we examine the manager's Talk, let's dig into a few important features of dreams. A dream isn't necessarily a goal, though a goal can be a dream. A goal usually has objective measurements, whereas a dream is an affective realization of a state of future events. People will seldom put their lives on the line for goals, but they will do so for the most compelling dreams. Like goals, however, dreams can trigger results-producing actions. When Thomas Jefferson wrote in the Declaration of Independence, "Governments derive their just powers from the consent of the governed," he was conveying not a goal (no government in Europe at that time was a democracy), but a dream that still motivates people around the world to take profound action.

Dreams aren't fantasies. Going to the mountain might be a dream, but having the mountain come to us is a fantasy. Dreams can be realized, fantasies can't. Focus on dreams, on what's objectively achievable, not on fantasies.

The most powerful dreams can be visualized. In fact, dreams are defining moments of the future. When you see your dream in your mind's eye, you're more likely to be motivated by it than if it's an abstract concept. For instance, the people who had the good-old-days dream reveled in the past, continually reminiscing about the people they knew and the jobs they had and hence were constantly reinforcing the strength of the old dream.

People hold to their dreams even in abject circumstances. If they lose their dreams, they can't be motivated.

Many people don't consciously realize what they dream, but that doesn't mean they're not influenced by their subconscious dream. A subconscious dream can motivate powerfully, getting people to act without understanding clearly why they're acting. Have the people you lead be fully conscious of the content and meaning of their dream, or risk having your organization's activities impeded by a dimly perceived yet nonetheless potent toxic dream.

Each dream has a price. It's one thing to think it, and another to do it. Know the price of the dream. Have them understand the price.

It's not easy to find out what they dream. If they don't trust you, they won't tell you what they dream, and if they don't think you can help them realize their dream, they won't trust you.

Dreams are usually positive, uplifting. "Hope," said Aristotle, "is a waking dream." The root of the word is in celebration: the Old English word "dream" means "joy, music, and noisemaking." But that positive, inspirational quality can have toxic effects on an organization as it did with the manager.

As to the manager's challenge, the fact that he came to realize that dreams are vital motivational triggers was a big step toward achieving his goals, as the vast majority of leaders know little about the power of dreams. The next step, of course, was to find out what they dreamed. In this case, he couldn't let a good-old-days dream stand. Transforming an old, toxic dream into a new, positive one is no quick, easy task. It's as difficult as changing recalcitrant people into cause leaders, but it can be done. Often, the best way is through the advice of that great commentator on leadership and human motivation, Plutarch. The ancient Greek biographer said that leaders change such people "by gentle usage to cure their angry and intractable tempers and bring them to order and discipline by the mildest and fairest means, and not treat them worse than gardeners do those wild plants, which, with care and attention, lose gradually the savageness of their nature, and bear excellent fruit."

Dreams do indeed bear fruit, excellent fruit if positive dreams, and bitter if toxic; and if one intends to change people's toxic dream into a positive one (i.e., have the people make the choice to change), one needs to apply "the mildest and fairest means"—in this case, Leadership Talks.

To have his audience choose to discard their old dream, he gave Leadership Talks predicated on their identifying their most pressing need, which turned out to be job security, and creating value by linking the solution to their dream (i.e., having them investigate whether returning to the good old days would boost or reduce job security). The answer for most of them—there were, as always, some who wouldn't comply with the analysis process—was that such a dream indeed hampered their ability to tackle the present challenges, and that to do so, they had to abandon the old dream and create a new one, whose realization would help them get consistently increased results. Only when their organization is experiencing a dramatic increase or decrease in results will the people be motivated to change their dream. If they think that their old, toxic dream brings the best solutions, you'll never change their dream. Only when the new dream provides them better solutions will they choose to change.

In this case, the change never materialized; in the midst of his efforts, the company underwent another restructuring, his newly patched-together department was split up, and he was promoted to head a division. However, he'd come a long way in recognizing the importance of dreams and applying the Leadership Talk to help change a toxic dream into a positive one—skills he could apply in other leadership venues.

I don't want it to seem that he easily applied the Leadership Talk processes, like sprinkling pixie dust and—poof!—they changed their dream. It took hard work on his part. For one thing, not all of them had the same dream, and for another, they were reluctant to let go of the old dream, even when the saw how it was impeding them. But we can't know who we are if we don't try to be better than we are. The best of our dreams are pathways to our better selves.

Belief

The **Issue:** The global reorganization

The **Talk:** In the hotel ballroom, the manufacturing leader got up in front of the global leadership council and used the defining moment of his growing up living and breathing the company through the franchise his father owned. He related how the experience of being a part of something that he was convinced was the best in the world defined his character and aspirations, and ultimately provided an inspiriting solution to their needs. He communicated necessary information, and also communicated the necessity for their having to be partners in seeing the reorganization through. But I see now that he gave essentially a speech, not a Leadership Talk, and the difference provides a lesson that goes right to the core of the Talk.

The problem wasn't in what he said, but in what I think failed to take place after he said it. After all, a speech is about speaking, but the Leadership Talk isn't just about talking, but about leading; it's about what happens through leading after the initial talking. Sure, many of the leaders in the ballroom might have been persuaded to commit to making the restructuring a success, but much more could have been done. I didn't have him fully understand that his communication wasn't just to the leaders in the ballroom, but to those leaders who weren't there, maybe the most important leaders of all, the many thousands of managers and small-unit leaders around the world. A cascading of such cause leaders needed to unfold; often, the highest multiplier of results is the lowest common denominator of small-unit leadership. Clearly, the unfolding couldn't have happened as a direct result of his speech. After all, he had to first get the leaders in the ballroom to choose to be cause leaders before the cascading could take effect. But he could have given a Leadership Talk to ignite a "leadership strategy." Most good leaders can develop, as this leader did, sound business strategies, but they miss out on creating a leadership strategy, a comprehensive, interlocking campaign of Leadership Talks to get grassroots, cause-leader commitment to execute the strategy. Unless that commitment saturates an organization through all functions and leadership levels, execution inevitably stumbles.

There was no leadership strategy. The cascading didn't happen—at least not from my perspective. For one thing, I was brought in as a speechwriter, not a leadership consultant, and that became a self-fulfilling prophecy. Also, I blame myself for it not happening, or at least for my not persuading some of the key leaders that it must. Though I had just about fully developed the Leadership Talk processes, I was still working out the means by which the Talks could saturate entire organizations in systematic, comprehensive ways. (Several years later, I described those means in my book *Results!Results!Results Getting More Faster.*) Further, at that time, my own company didn't have the infrastructure to carry out a deeply saturating global campaign in one of the world's largest companies. And finally, I too had been caught up in the leader's fallacy—I thought that my passion would be reciprocated. So, after his speech, I didn't follow up. I should have had him and his colleagues see that the reorganization itself wasn't enough to get the results they wanted—as complicated, exacting, and comprehensive as the endeavor was. I should have had them see the second step that I talked about regarding another major global company in the preface of this book. That step would have involved enlisting an army of small-unit leaders around the world to be cause leaders for the reorganization.

Today, I do things much differently: I make sure leaders understand that major communications like that are truly Leadership Talks that are linked to a leadership strategy that supports their business strategy.

Action

The Issue: Speed

The Talk: We might not be able to change circumstances, but we can always change choice. The leaders in her organization were taking a lot of action for speed, but speed wasn't happening because they were choosing to take the wrong actions. Her potential cause leader was the right person to take the right actions. He had the skills, knowledge and contacts, but had until then been a reluctant employee who was having personal difficulties with some of his coworkers and wanted to be transferred out of the department. She knew he wouldn't choose to be her cause leader unless she dealt with his immediate need to transfer. Applying the Leadership Talk principle that the best solutions come from the leadership of the people themselves, she challenged him to be his own transfer cause-leader. They put together an informal leadership contract spelling out specific actions he would take to effect that transfer. When he learned that the positions he wanted to transfer to in other departments were closed to him, he figured he'd better forget about getting out and start focusing on staying, protecting his job and career. With this new need in mind, they drew up a new leadership contract dealing with his being the cause leader to engender speed in the order-to-remittance process. Because of his special skills and knowledge, he proposed and carried out leadership actions that were far more effective than any actions she had thought of. She supported his leadership by removing obstacles to it (helping him work out the difficulties he had with his coworkers), providing training and tools, and helping him get the recognition that he sought. Through his persistent leadership, she got the speed she sought.

Glossary

Action—within the context of the Leadership Talk, the physical activity of people seeking results. There is right and wrong action. Right action is what helps get more results, faster, continually; wrong action doesn't. It's as simple as that, but of course, there's more to it: right action has specific characteristics. Right action is actual physical action. When you link people's precise physical action to results, you see those people and the results in powerful new ways. Right action is purposeful. When your audience takes action, they should be clearly conscious what action they're taking, and why. Right action is honest—don't trick people into taking action. Right action is meaningful. Your audience must want to take that action because *they* want to, not because you told them to; they'll usually want to when that action leads to solutions to the problems of their needs. In addition, there's action that flows from two different sources: the leadership contract, which triggers long-term leadership action, and the call to action, which triggers immediate action (see doing vs. leading).

Action Leadership—a comprehensive system of principles and interlocking processes that aim at motivating people and their organizations to achieve more results, faster, continually. The Leadership Talk and the Results Process form the two main parts of Action Leadership, which is covered in my book, *Results!Results!Results! Getting More Faster*.

Action process—the purpose of which is to have your audience take right action for right results. 1. Describe: Have your audience describe the leadership actions that they will take to achieve more results faster, continually. 2. Test: Test the results using your own methodologies or applying the SAMMER test. 3. Contract: Come to an agreement on what those actions will be (see leadership contract). 4. Support: Detail how you will support their leadership. This support can include removing barriers, providing accelerators to their leadership, and giving them special training and resources. 5. Monitor and evaluate: Describe how their leadership actions will be monitored and evaluated.

Audience—that person or persons whom we want to motivate to be our cause leader(s). Your audience can be one person, thousands of people or any number in between. It can be your boss, your team members, the people who report to you, your teenager, your coworkers. It doesn't matter how many or how few people you speak to; and it doesn't matter whom you speak to; you can always deliver a Leadership Talk.

Belief—The second trigger in the three-trigger motivational process. You can't give a Leadership Talk without believing strongly in what you're saying. Furthermore, your belief, in its full strength and content, must also be imparted to your audience. This is done through the motivational transfer (see defining moment).

Bridging the poles—Often, you will encounter an audience whose members comprise two opposite poles of an issue. In that case, it's best to speak to each single major problem of the opposing audience segments. But always do more: Speak to what bridges the poles. Do that by raising the stakes. Let's say one part of the audience wants to go right. The other part of the audience wants to go left. So you speak to one part of the audience about going right. Then speak to the other part of the audience about going left. Finally, raise the stakes. Talk about how disastrous—or necessary—heir wanting to go in opposite directions is to your overall goals. Develop a common, overriding goal that they can both march toward. Opposite poles in an audience can usually be bridged—but not until you first acknowledge each pole.

Call to action—words or demonstrations that prompt people to take action for results. *Call* comes from an Old English word meaning "to shout." A call to action, then, is a "shout for action." Implicit in the concept is urgency and forcefulness, but leaders often mistake the call to action for an order. Within the context of the Leadership Talk, a call to action is not an order. Leave that for the order leader. Leaders also mistake the call as theirs to give. The best call to action isn't the leader's to give—it's the audience's to give. It's the audience's to give to themselves. A Leadership Talk's call to action is a trigger for the audience to motivate themselves to take action. The most effective call to action then is not from the leader to the audience but from the audience to the audience. The right action triggered by the call to action takes place immediately in your presence.

Cascading of cause leaders—the act of saturating an organization with an expanding network of cause leaders and their activities. In order to insure that organizational goals are continually kept in mind and that people are not taking leadership any way they see fit, the actions of cause leaders must be grounded in leadership contracts.

Cause—a higher order of aspiration than simply a goal. The Leadership Talk is not aimed at having people be "goal leaders" but cause leaders; because getting more results faster, continually is a matter of being committed to a cause. This is not to say that there will not be goals within a cause. Inevitably, there are; for one usually obtains goals in leading a cause. Goals emerge as their cause leadership unfolds. However, don't let these definitions deter you from having people make the choice to be your cause leaders. After all, the terms "cause" and "goals" are merely words. If your audience is willing to commit themselves to take leadership for a cause or a goal or however you define the objective, definitions should not stand in your way. The point is that when we differentiate between a cause and a goal, we can challenge people to a higher leadership calling, and thus clarify their aspiration and their assessment of the price that they must pay to lead.

Cause leader—people whom we want to lead our cause to achieve more results, faster, continually. You can't order someone to be a cause leader. It's a matter of their free choice. Furthermore, when people make the choice to be cause leaders, they must be clearly conscious that leadership action is required. That's best done by agreeing on a leadership contract. The most effective way of motivating people to make the choice to be your cause leaders is through the Leadership Talk.

Change—in terms of the Leadership Talk, the best way to deal with change is to motivate people to be cause leaders to take leadership of change. You cannot have such motivation happen unless you first identify what is changing for your audience and have them see that their leadership is the best way for them to solve the problem in the change.

Critical confluence—the union of our cause and our cause leaders' cause. The critical confluence is a much deeper and richer relationship than the self-limiting win/win; for unlike win/win, the critical confluence is an on-going relationship process from which flow mutually beneficial expectations and solutions.

Defining moment—that living moment of ours or of others that changed us in some small or large way and that provides an experiential solution to an important problem of our audience. The defining moment is not an analogy. It differs from an analogy by emotion, intensity, and drama. It is not a story. It differs from a story by its being a moment of pure experience. The defining moment is communicated to the audience by describing the physical facts that gave one the emotion. It is one of the most effective ways to generate the motivational transfer. When the leader's defining moment becomes a solution to the needs of the audience, the Leadership Talk has a great chance of success.

Doing vs. leading—doing is the act of simply accomplishing tasks. It is contrasted with leading, which is a higher order of action and accomplishment, involving more initiative, energy, insight, and persuasiveness. The function of the Leadership Talk is to challenge people to lead, not do.

Dream—In regard to the Leadership Talk, a dream is a powerful expectation that promotes strong commitment. When giving Leadership

Talks, you need to identify the dreams of your audience in terms of their positive or negative power regarding the results you intend to achieve. Only a trusted leader can help people reshape their dreams. Reshape people's negative or toxic dreams into positive and advantageous ones by creating value in their jobs and in their relationship with you. Create value for them by constantly giving Leadership Talks. If they lose their dreams, they can't be motivated. Your leadership won't transform them if you have a low opinion of, and low expectations for, their dream, and if they're convinced that you can't help them attain that dream. Have the people you lead be fully conscious of the content and meaning of their dream, or risk having your organization's activities be impeded by a dimly perceived yet nonetheless potent dream. Even if you do all the seven other questions and answers right, you can undo your motivational relationship by stumbling in the dream section. Today, people are trying to sell us dreams in the forms of products, services, movies, lotteries, and commercials. Dream-sold, we've become dream-cynical. We risk disheartening people if we oversell the dream. Still, let's dream! Just as people even in abject circumstances must dream, so people become dispirited if they don't dream and you don't dream with them. Graffiti on a Paris wall during the 1968 student rebellion said, "Be realistic: Do the impossible!" Dreams are ultimate reality.

Eight Needs Questions—the answers help the leader identify the audience's emotional reality. 1: What's changing for your audience? 2: Whom would the audience rather have speaking to them besides you? 3: What action does the audience want to take? 4: What does the audience feel? 5: What does the audience fear? 6: What's the audience's major problem? 7: What makes the audience angry? 8: What does the audience dream?

Emotion—an affective state of the mind and body that stimulates motivation and hence action. Emotion is one aspect of the need/emotion/problem continuum. The Leadership Talk recognizes that emotions are tools to get results. To motivate people to be our cause leaders, we must see their emotions in their need, and then work on bringing solutions to the problems of their need / emotions. Their emotions are their reality. They won't listen to your reality until you validate theirs. When you speak of what's authentic to people, to their emotions and what triggers them, you become authentic to them, not a caricature of a leader, which is too easy for them to dismiss or despise. Be aware of easy and hard emotions: easy emotions are linked to people saying that those other people have to change; hard emotions are linked to people saying that they themselves must change. Challenge people to take action from their hard emotions.

Emotional talking points—also called the needs talking points. These are the key structural headings of the Leadership Talk. They derive from the answers to the eight needs questions. By making their needs / emotions the headings, we begin developing the critical confluence.

Experience—In terms of the Leadership Talk, experience is a vehicle for achieving the motivational transfer. When the leader's experience becomes the audience's experience, the audience is more likely to choose to be cause leaders (see defining moment). The lasting purpose of experience is character enrichment.

Face-to-face talk—a primary method to motivate others to take action for results. Powerful motivational bonds develop between speaker and audience when the audience understands that the speaker is in tune with their needs. Face-to-face interaction promotes such relationships.

Fear—In terms of the Leadership Talk, a fear is a key problem of most audiences whom you want to motivate to be your cause leaders. People usually experience some degree of fear (mostly fear of failure) in organizational endeavors. In fact, if they don't experience fear, the endeavor may not be important enough for them to want to go to the trouble of being your cause leader.

Good-old-days dream—the dream of an organization's participants that the organization was a better place to work in the past.

Information—In terms of the Leadership Talk, communicating information is one way to effect the motivational transfer. However, the purpose of the Leadership Talk isn't simply to communicate information, but to communicate information in a way that your audience makes the choice to be your cause leaders.

Killer gap—A motivational gap so strong that if not closed it will "kill" our chances of getting the results we need.

Leader's fallacy—the leader's conviction that the audience automatically reciprocates his or her motivation. You pierce the fallacy by answering the eight needs questions and engaging your audience in the action process.

Leader/leadership—In the context of the Leadership Talk, the people who motivate others to take leadership action for more results, faster, continually. The word "leadership" comes from an old Norse word root meaning "to make go." Indeed, leadership is about making things go—making people go, making organizations go, but many leaders fail to see who actually makes what go. They often believe that they must make things go, that if people must go from point A to point B, for example, that they must order them to go. But order leadership founders when people need to get more results, faster, continually. A new kind of leadership must be cultivated, that aims not to order others to go from point A to point B, but to motivate them to want take leadership in going from A to B. The leader's effectiveness is measured not just by the effectiveness of his or her leadership but by the effectiveness of the leadership of the people he or she leads.

Leadership contract—an unwritten or written agreement (usually informal) between the leader and the cause leaders, detailing the specific leadership actions the audience will take to achieve more results, faster, continually. The first step in developing the contract is to have the audience propose what leadership actions should be taken to accomplish the results. The next step is to apply a testing method, such as the SAMMER test, to the results. Then, come to agreement as to what those actions will be. (The leader can always veto any actions the cause leaders propose.) Next, come to agreement as to how that leadership will be supported. Finally, come to agreement as to how the actions will be evaluated and monitored.

Leadership strategy—an overall plan or series of communications and person-to-person interactions for obtaining cause leaders throughout an entire organization and having those cause leaders take action that achieves more results, faster, continually. The most effective way of planning and carrying out a leadership strategy is by employing Leadership Talks. Most good leaders can develop business strategies, but neglect to develop a leadership strategy for motivating leaders of all ranks and functions to be cause leaders for that strategy. Without a leadership strategy supporting a business strategy, the execution of the latter can founder.

Leadership Talk—a means of communicating, whose purpose is to motivate the audience to choose to be one's cause leader in achieving more results, faster, continually. It involves not just talking to people, but talking *with* people and listening to people; often the most effective Leadership Talk is given from the audience to the speaker (see Listening Leadership Talk). A Leadership Talk is based on the three-trigger motivational process. Before one can give a Leadership Talk, one must say yes to the process questions "Do I know the needs of the audience? Can I bring deep belief to what I say? Can I have the audience take action?" A Leadership Talk isn't a pep talk. It's not about bands playing, flags waving, and people cheering, but about deepening and clarifying human relationships through action and results. Leaders who don't continually give Leadership Talks are always overpaid; leaders who do are always underpaid.

Logical response—a motivational element that necessitates a logical solution to the problem of the emotion. The logical response includes an analysis of the problem in the need and the stakes, and a process to solve the problem.

Major problem—the single significant problem that defines an audience's need.

More results, faster, continually—a cause-leader imperative. Leaders do nothing more important than get results. When they're getting more results, faster, continually, they have the best chance of controlling their destiny before someone else does. More results, faster, continually should be achieved not by having people work harder and faster but by constantly giving Leadership Talks that move them to slow down and work smarter.

Motivation—the stimulus that impels people to make the choice to take physical action. In the context of the Leadership Talk, motivation isn't what people think or feel, but what they physically do. We can't motivate our audience; they must motivate themselves. Emotion triggers motivation. People aren't motivated unless their emotions are engaged. Motivation best takes place through face-to-face talk. The four levels of motivating people to take action for results, in ascending order of importance: 1. They listen. 2. They see. 3. They do. 4. They lead. An indifferent leader can't.

Motivational element—the six elements that make up a Leadership Talk—emotion, validation, defining moment, logical response, support, action—the purpose of which is to motivate them (i.e., have the audience motivate themselves) to be cause leaders for achieving more results, faster, continually. The elements comprise the content of the Talk; the talking points comprise its structure. One needn't use all the motivational elements in each Talk, though need, logical response, and action are necessary.

Motivational gap—the gap between the motivation we feel in regard to obtaining certain results and the motivation the audience feels. We close motivational gaps (i.e., we come to have our audience be as motivated as we are), by giving Leadership Talks. Here is a process for closing gaps. 1. Select which side of the gap you want to focus on—the side that will get results. (Don't necessarily focus on your side of the gap. Their side might be more important for getting results, or bridging the gap may be more important.) For example, they want to walk, you need for them to run. In this case, "run" is going to get you the best results. Focus on the run side. 2. Recast your selection as a problem. For example, your audience doesn't want to run. 3. Precisely define that problem by breaking it down into its *defining characteristics,* the concrete factors that make up the problem. For example, you may think that they don't want to run because they're lazy. From your perspective, their laziness is the problem's defining characteristic. But from their perspective, they might not want to run because they don't have the proper running shoes; they don't feel they're in shape; they fear they'll fail—same problem, different defining characteristics. 4. You and they must agree on the defining characteristics of the problem. If you tell them they're lazy when, from their standpoint, their major concerns are shoes, physical conditioning, and failure, you can't motivate them. You must agree on the defining characteristics of the problem, or you can't close the motivational gap. 5. Close the gap by using the action process, paying particular attention to the leadership contract in which you challenge them to come up with solutions to their problem. For example, tell them you'll give them information on how to run well, and equipment to run well, and that you'll train them and put them through conditioning exercises, practice sessions, and competitions. Be constantly engaged in gap recognition and gap closing. A motivational gap isn't necessarily a stakes gap, but a stakes gap is always a motivational gap.

Motivational transfer—the transferring of the leader's strong belief to the audience. A leader should be motivated; if not, he or she won't be leading for long. But the key challenge of the Leadership Talk isn't just that motivation is the leader's to have, but the audience's to receive. The motivational transfer takes place only in the realm of the audience's needs. The transfer can be effected in three ways: through information, structure, and experience (see defining moment).

Motivational transfer process—the means by which we effect the motivational transfer by bringing our experiences into the hearts of our audience. This is more than simply communicating our experience. It involves an experiential interaction. 1. Recognize the importance of bringing deep belief to your talking interaction, and that you must transfer belief to your audience. 2. Identify the experience that gave you that belief. 3. Transform the experience into a defining moment. 4. Transfer by describing those facts to your audience. The defining moment must play like a movie clip, a moment of physical action, in the minds of your audience. The motivational transfer happens when the communicated experience furnishes a solution to the audience's need.

Needs—conditions marked by the lack of some essential element, the needs of your audience as defined by the answers to the eight needs questions. In the context of the Leadership Talk, needs are problems seeking solutions. Every need involves an emotional response. We motivate people to choose to be our cause leaders only by working in the realm of their need(see need / emotion / problem continuum and critical confluence).

Needs analysis / needs questions—(see Eight Needs Questions).

Needs talking points—the major headings of a Leadership Talk. These are always the audience's needs, not yours. By making their needs the major headings of your Talk, you promote the critical confluence. The talking points derive from the eight needs questions.

Need / emotion / problem continuum—every need embodies an emotion, and that need / emotion is a problem seeking a solution. When you understand the emotion in the need and the problem in the need / emotion, you're better positioned to deliver a Leadership Talk. If you're simply giving orders to people, you don't have to understand the continuum. But if you want to have your audience choose to be your cause leaders, you must understand each aspect of it. That understanding provides critical focus when challenging your audience to take leadership of the solutions to the problems in the needs / emotions. If you're not helping them bring solutions to the problems of their needs, you're not their leader, even though you have nominal authority over them.

Order leadership—directing people to accomplish tasks. The word "order" comes from a Latin root meaning to order or arrange threads in a woof, which gives an idea of the relationship between the order leader and those being ordered. Order leadership is the cocaine of leadership: powerful in its immediate effects but habit forming and ultimately destructive. Order leadership may achieve more results, faster—but not *continually*. That's because people may respond to orders short term, but over the long term, their being constantly ordered dispirits them, stifles them, and makes them resentful. It's far better to challenge people to take leadership to get results than to simply order them.

Presentation—a method of speaking primarily focused on persuading people through the communication of information. The Leadership Talk is not a presentation methodology, though it may have elements of such a methodology to help support it.

Price—in terms of the Leadership Talk, the expenditure of time, effort, and resources to get results. You and your potential or actual cause leaders must identify the price they'll have to pay to be cause leaders. This goes beyond simply understanding; it involves appreciation, that is, knowing the price's value in regard to your need and theirs.

Problem—in terms of the need / emotion / problem continuum, problem helps you focus on how to bring value to the audience so they make the choice to lead your cause. When you identify your audience's problem in their need, you've gone a long way toward getting cause leaders.

Process—physical or mental steps directed toward getting results. Process isn't procedure or policy: procedure is a prescribed course or method of action that we generally follow to the letter; policies are governing mechanisms for procedures and processes.

Resources—works on both sides of the Leadership Talk equation. On one side, when giving a Leadership Talk, you should understand the resources your audience is willing to expend to achieve more results, faster, continually. The most difficult resource to get from them is usually their leadership. On the other side, when they've committed to leading your cause, you should provide the resources to help them.

Results—the consequences of actions. Most leaders strive diligently to get the wrong results—either by achieving wrong results outright, or by targeting the right results in the wrong ways. Since the Leadership Talk aims at having cause leaders achieve not just average results but more results faster, continually, those results must be constantly tested (see SAMMER test) and constantly increased. Whatever results have been achieved, more results can be achieved—as long as you're applying Leadership Talks.

Results process—a process of Action Leadership that promotes the exhaustive, systematic dissemination of Leadership Talks throughout all functions and levels of organizations. The process is: 1: Define results. 2: Define cause leader needs. 3. Define performance. 4. Define the vision. 5. Define processes. 6. Get results. 7. Step up results. 8. Repeat process. The results process is covered in my book, *Results!Results!Results! Getting more, faster.*

Right action—the action that achieves not just average results but more results, faster, continually (see action).

Root emotions—the emotions that are at the core of needs. Often, when answering the needs questions, the first answer that comes to mind isn't the most effective, it being too quickly and easily arrived at. Answers that get to the root of the matter are often realized only after rigorous analysis, including the discarding of superficial explanations. However, as you become skilled at identifying the emotional component of the needs / emotion / problem continuum, trust your intuitive insights. With practice, you'll find that such insights become increasingly accurate and powerful.

SAMMER Test—helps identify and determine right results. Results should be Sizable; they must be more, faster, continually results. Results must be Achievable, challenging but not impossible. Results must be Meaningful; your cause leaders must be passionately committed to achieving them. Results must be Measurable; you should be able to quantify them to provide a standard of value, though this might not be possible in all cases. Results must be Ethical; you achieve them with integrity and report on them honestly. Results must be Repeatable; they should be springboards for even more results.

Solution—The word "solution" comes from a Latin root meaning, "to set free." How fitting this is for the Leadership Talk; through solutions, your audience is "set free" to take leadership for your cause. In fact, if they don't think their leadership will provide solutions to their needs (not yours), they won't take such leadership. Solutions must strengthen and promote the critical confluence.

Stakes gap—the gap between your view of what the stakes are in the leadership challenge you're confronting, and your potential or actual cause leaders' view of the same stakes. Stakes gaps are linked to motivational gaps.

Status quo—the existing situation. In terms of the Leadership Talk, our recognizing what's changing in the seemingly static status quo is a tool for more results, faster, continually. Further, the status quo will continually try to frustrate its transformation, in particular the transformation that must achieve more results, faster, continually. The status quo is always wrong.

Structure—a key factor in promoting the motivational transfer. Your Leadership Talk must make sense to your audience. Their emotional commitment to take action for you stems from their logical assessment of your Talk. If they can't logically connect what you say with who they are, they're unlikely to choose to be your cause leaders. Structure advances the logic of the Talk.

Support—a motivational element whose function is to support the leadership of cause leaders. In the context of the Leadership Talk, support is indispensable. Order leadership traditionally entails leaders coming up with solutions, then ordering people to carry them out. Instead, the Leadership Talk has leaders motivate people to choose to be cause leaders who take leadership for more results, faster, continually. Leadership, then, should be assessed not just by how effectively the leader leads, but also, and more importantly, by how effectively cause leaders lead. Supporting those cause leaders entails removing obstacles to their leadership and providing accelerators for it, such as special training and resources. Therefore, support becomes the most important thing a leader can do, aside from getting cause leaders for more results, faster, continually.

Sympathy vs. motivation—Sympathizing with the people you lead isn't motivating them. When you sympathize, you engage in a harmony of feeling. But when you motivate people, you're challenging them to take action that gets results; often, you're having them do what they don't want to do. When Italian patriot General Giuseppe Garibaldi said to his soldiers, "I offer neither pay nor quarters nor provisions. I offer hunger, thirst, forced marches, battles, and death. Let him who loves his country with his heart, not with his lips, follow me," he wasn't sympathizing with them, but motivating them (i.e., having them choose to follow).

The Listening Leadership Talk—The difference between leaders is ears. Your best Leadership Talks don't come only from your mouth, but out of the mouths of your audience. Your listening can trigger those Talks. Ask the needs questions and listen to your audience give you the answers. Their answers can be your Leadership Talk. Their answers are their motivational triggers. Don't just listen. The Listening Leadership Talk isn't free association. They shouldn't be all over the map when speaking. Instead, use the needs questions as a framework and a stimulant for listening. Make sure they stay within your guidelines, by constantly having them return to their identified needs (see #1 of Interactive Talks).

Three-trigger motivational process—the foundation process of the Leadership Talk, based on three questions: What does the audience need? Can we bring deep belief to what we say? Can we have the audience take action? If you can't answer yes to all three, you can't give a Leadership Talk. The questions aren't stumbling blocks, but steppingstones; if you can't answer yes, work the Leadership Talk processes until you can.

Unified field theory of leadership success—a series of propositions that describes the underpinning principles of the Leadership Talk: 1. Organizational success is a function of leaders directing those organizations to achieve results. 2. Leaders direct organizations to achieve results by having people get those results. 3. The best way to have people get results is not to order them but to motivate them. 4. Motivation is physical action. 5. Motivation isn't what leaders do to people, but what people do to themselves. 6. Motivation is triggered by emotion. 6. Motivation best happens through face-to-face speech.

Validation—identifying and agreeing with your audience on the need/emotion/problem continuum and its relevance or irrelevance in getting results. Without such agreement, you'll likely fail to have your audience choose to be your cause leaders. Validation helps develop the critical confluence.

Index